GLOBAPHOBIA

GLOBAPHOBIA
Confronting Fears about Open Trade

Gary Burtless   Robert Z. Lawrence
            Robert E. Litan   Robert J. Shapiro

Brookings Institution
Progressive Policy Institute
Twentieth Century Fund

Globaphobia: Confronting Fears about Open Trade may be ordered from
  Brookings Institution Press
  1775 Massachusetts Avenue, N.W.
  Washington, D.C. 20036
  Tel: 1-800-275-1447 or 202-797-6258
  Fax: 202-797-6195

Library of Congress Cataloging-in-Publication data

Globaphobia : confronting fears about open trade / by Gary Burtless
. . . [et al.].
    p.   cm.
  "The Brookings Institution [and] The Progressive Policy Institute [and] the
Twentieth Century Fund."
  Includes bibliographical references and index.
  ISBN 0-8157-1190-5 (alk.paper).–ISBN 0-8157-1189-1 (pbk.: alk. paper)
  1. International economic integration.   2. International economic
integration—Social aspects.   3. Free trade.   4. Competition,
International.   5. Free trade—United States.   6. United
States—Commercial Policy.   7. Foreign trade and employment—United
States.   I. Burtless, Gary T., 1950–   II. Progressive Policy
Institute (U.S.)   III. Twentieth Century Fund.
  HF1418.5 .G582 1998
  382'.0973—ddc21   98-8916
                                                                        ·   CIP

9 8 7 6 5 4 3 2 1

The paper used in this publication meets the minimum requirements of the
American National Standard for Information Sciences—Permanence of Paper
for Printed Library Materials, ANSI Z39-48-1984.

Typeset in Sabon and Futura

Composition by Harlowe Typography, Inc.
Cottage City, Maryland

Printed by R. R. Donnelley and Sons Co.
Crawfordsville, Indiana

Title page illustration by Claude Goodwin
New York, New York

The Brookings Institution is an independent organization devoted to nonpartisan research, education, and publication in economics, government, foreign policy, and the social sciences generally. The principal purposes of the Institution, which traces its foundations to 1916, are to aid in the development of sound public policies and to promote public understanding of issues of national importance.

The Progressive Policy Institute (PPI) is a center for policy innovation that develops alternatives to the conventional left-right debate. Founded in 1989, the Institute is fashioning a public philosophy for the twenty-first century by adapting America's progressive tradition of individual liberty, equal opportunity, and civic obligation to the challenges of the Information Age. The Progressive Policy Institute is a project of the Progressive Foundation.

The Twentieth Century Fund/The Century Foundation sponsors and supervises timely analyses of economic policy, foreign affairs, and domestic political issues. Not-for-profit and nonpartisan, the Fund was founded in 1919 and endowed by Edward A. Filene.

FOREWORD

It is one of the paradoxes of our modern age. America has been leading the world to encourage more integration of national economies. Yet just as we appear to be succeeding, increasing numbers of Americans appear to be expressing growing doubts or worries about this process of "globalization."

Several factors seem to be responsible for this unusual coincidence of developments. Although the American economy has experienced one of its longest peacetime expansions in the 1990s, many Americans have been left behind, with their real incomes not much improved, or even lower than what they were earning a decade ago. In addition, the turbulence in labor and financial markets has generated uncertainty for many of those who otherwise have fared quite well. In this environment, globalization becomes an easy scapegoat for unwelcome economic news.

The four authors of this important book seek to demonstrate the fallacies that underpin this "globaphobia." They do so in clear prose, with numerous illustrations, and in the process, bring to life some of the abstract concepts that are familiar to economists, but not to many members of the public. In their view, buttressed by much economic evidence, globalization continues to benefit, rather than harm, the American economy. To be sure, there are losers—a fact that some economists and political leaders have underestimated and underplayed. That is why the authors recommend a more effective safety net that eases the transition of workers displaced by the diverse forces of economic change, including trade.

Collectively, the authors bring much research and analytical expertise to their task. Gary Burtless, a senior fellow in the Economic Studies program at Brookings, is one of the nation's leading specialists in labor economics. Robert Z. Lawrence, holder of the New Century Chair in International Trade and Economics at Brookings and the Albert L. Williams Chair of International Trade and Investment at the John F. Kennedy School of Government at Harvard, is recognized as one of the nation's foremost empirical trade economists. Robert E. Litan, director of Economic Studies and holder of the Cabot Family Chair in Economics at Brookings, has written widely on a variety of subjects, including trade and finance, and served recently in two high-level positions in the Clinton administration. And Robert J. Shapiro, a founder and former vice president of the Progressive Policy Institute and, at this writing, the administration's nominee to be under secretary of the Department of Commerce for economic affairs, also is one of the nation's leading economic policy analysts.

This book is the product of collaboration between the Brookings Institution, the Progressive Policy Institute, and the Twentieth Century Fund. The authors and this project have benefited from the generous funding, support, and advice of Harry Freeman, a long-time member of the Brookings Council and a former executive vice president of the American Express Company.

The authors are grateful for the many helpful comments and suggestions provided by readers of earlier versions of this manuscript, including Greg Anrig Jr., Richard Cooper, William Frenzel, Gary Hufbauer, David Richardson, and Charles Schultze.

At the same time, the authors remain fully responsible for the views expressed in the book, which do not necessarily reflect the views of the trustees, officers, or other staff members of the Brookings Institution, the Progressive Policy Institute, or the Twentieth Century Fund.

Finally, the authors appreciate the editing assistance of Tanjam Jacobson and Deborah Styles, the excellent research assistance of Steve Baron, verification by Cynthia Iglesias and Helen Kim, the administrative support of Anita Whitlock, and index preparation by Julia Petrakis.

Michael H. Armacost
President, The Brookings Institution

Richard Leone
President, The Twentieth Century Fund

Will Marshall
President, Progressive Policy Institute

February 1998

CONTENTS

CHAPTER 1 INTRODUCTION

To some, the performance of the U.S. economy since 1992 has been the best in a generation. In the summer of 1997, when the economy had expanded for more than five years, Federal Reserve Board chairman Alan Greenspan called this performance extraordinary. A few years earlier, then secretary of Labor Robert Reich had coined the label "Goldilocks economy"—neither too hot (with accelerating inflation) nor too cold (with rising unemployment).

Reich's term accurately describes the country's economic performance in recent years. Figure 1-1 sums up the good news of the 1990s: an unemployment rate falling steadily to its lowest level in more than twenty-five years; low and stable inflation; and stock prices far higher than at the beginning of the decade (despite some nervous jitters toward the end of 1997).

To others, however, the economy looks quite different: very kind to a few at the top, but barely rewarding for many in the middle, and a continuing nightmare for those at the bottom. Figure 1-2 illustrates the economic bad news:

- Notwithstanding the expansion in the 1990s, the wages (excluding fringe benefits) of the typical worker have barely grown since 1973, after steadily advancing about 2¼ percent a year over the previous twenty-five years.

Figure 1-1. The Good News

Unemployment rate is low

Percent unemployed

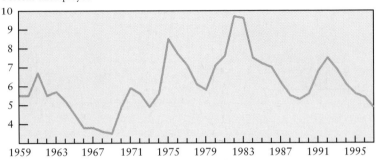

Inflation is moderate

Annual percentage change[a]

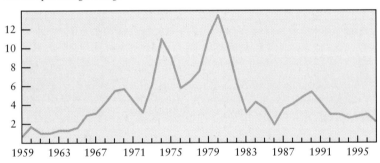

Dow Jones industrials hits new highs[b]

Index value

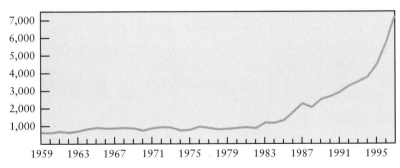

Source: Council of Economic Advisers (1997).
a. U.S. Consumer Price Index.
b. Annual average of daily closing prices.

Figure 1-2. The Bad News

Real wage growth has fallen

Annual percentage change

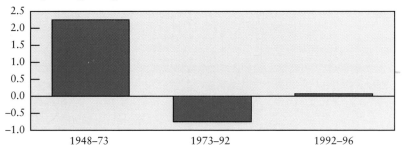

Lowest paid workers are worse off[a]

Percentage change[b]

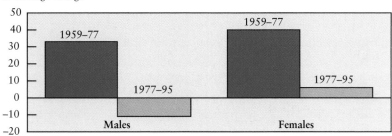

Family inequality is rising

Income ratio: top/bottom[c]

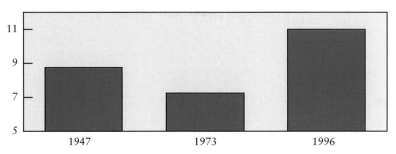

Source: Council of Economic Advisers (1991, 1997); and Gary Burtless's calculations based on decennial census and Current Population Surveys (March files).
a. Workers in bottom quintile of earnings distribution of 25–58 year-old, full-time, year-round workers.
b. Real annual earnings.
c. Average income in top quintile/Average income in bottom quintile.

- Men at the very bottom of the income distribution have actually suffered a sizable *drop* in their wages, while wage growth has disappeared for women at the bottom.
- The fact that well-paid Americans have continued to do well alongside the economic stagnation or deterioration of those not so fortunate has generated resentment over growing inequality.
- And, not shown in the figure but widely recognized is the anxiety of many middle class workers, who face the threat of being "downsized" or "reengineered." Watching their friends or neighbors lose jobs, they fear that they will be next.

The Dr. Jekyll–Mr. Hyde character of the U.S. economy cries out for explanation. One answer heard with increasing frequency in the halls of Congress, on talk shows, and perhaps also at dinner tables in homes across the country, is that "globalization"—the increasing economic linkage between the United States and other nations—is the main reason for the bad economic news just described. The logic behind this explanation is seductive. Figure 1-3 identifies three measures of globalization that have increased significantly since the early 1970s, when the adverse trends shown in figure 1-2 began. Imports have increased, not just absolutely, but in relation to the size of the economy, arguably placing strong pressure on the wages and jobs of U.S. workers. At the same time, American companies have significantly increased their investments abroad, which some critics believe has led to the export of American jobs and downward pressure on the wages of workers left behind. Moreover, the share of the U.S. population that consists of immigrants has nearly doubled during the past twenty-five years, further weakening the bargaining power of less-skilled Americans.

The fate of the U.S. economy has become increasingly linked with the economies of other nations for two reasons. One is well known and is, in fact, the result of deliberate policy. Since the end of the World War II, nations around the world, led by the United States, have been steadily lowering trade barriers—in recent cases, unilaterally. Average tariffs imposed by high-income countries like the United States have dropped from over 40 percent to just 6 percent, while barriers to ser-

Figure 1-3. Common Measures of Globalization

Goods and services imports

Percent of GDP

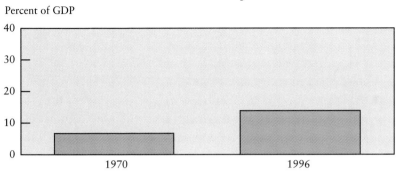

Cumulative U.S. direct investment abroad[a]

Percent of GDP

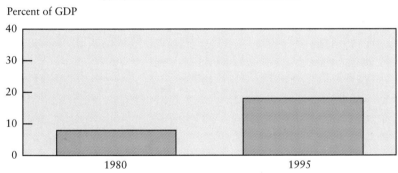

Immigrants

Percent of U.S. population

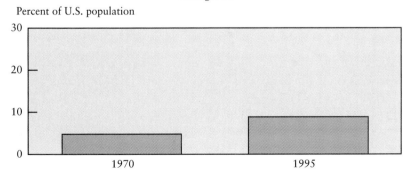

Sources: Council of Economic Advisers (1987, 1997); *Statistical Abstract of the United States,* 1984, 1988, 1997.
a. Historical cost basis.

vices trade have come down. Many countries have negotiated free trade agreements with their neighbors.

The other force behind globalization is one over which politicians have little or no control: the continuing progress of technology. Faster and bigger airplanes move people and goods more quickly and cheaply. The cost of communication, fueled by a revolution in computer and materials technologies, continues to plummet. Although most investment stays at home, large pools of liquid capital nonetheless flow around the world at a quickening pace in search of the best returns, as the Asian currency crisis of late 1997 vividly demonstrated.

Whatever the reasons behind it, globalization has aroused concern and outright hostility among some in the United States. Both were much in evidence in the fall of 1997, during the tense debate in Congress over the extension of "fast-track" trade negotiating authority for the president and in the ultimate decision to postpone a vote on the issue until some time in 1998. Critics of globalization are not limited to well-known figures in the three major political parties—Patrick Buchanan, Richard Gephardt, and Ross Perot. Opinion surveys show that at least half of the American population believes that "globalization"—whatever people assume the term means—does more harm than good and that expanded trade will lead to lower wages for American workers. These views no doubt help to explain why many polls show most Americans opposed to new free trade agreements. A similar, if not greater, degree of hostility to world economic integration is common in Europe.

We have written this book to demonstrate that the fear of globalization—or "globaphobia"—rests on very weak foundations. We do not dispute that the American economy, in particular, has a half full–half empty character. This is plain from figures 1-1 and 1-2. In the pages that follow, we argue that the surface appeal of globaphobia has nonetheless led many American voters and policymakers astray in a number of respects.

First, the United States globalized rapidly during the golden years before 1973, when productivity and wages were growing briskly and inequality was shrinking, demonstrating that living standards can advance at a healthy rate while the United States increases its links with the rest of the world. In any event, it is useful to keep in mind that the U.S. economy is no more globalized today—measured by the share of trade in its total output—than it was *before World War I*.

Second, even though globalization harms some American workers, the protectionist remedies suggested by some trade critics are, at best, short-term palliatives and, at worst, harmful to the interests of the broad class of workers that they are designed to help. Sheltering U.S. firms from imports may grant some workers a short reprieve from wage cuts or downsizing. But protection dulls the incentives of workers and firms to innovate and stay abreast of market developments. As a result, its benefits for individual workers and firms are often temporary. Indeed, protection invites foreign exporters to leap trade barriers by building plants in this country—as foreign manufacturers of automobiles, automobile parts, film, and other products have done. We are not criticizing this result: the United States has a strong national interest in attracting foreign investors, who typically bring technologies and management practices that ultimately yield higher wages and living standards for U.S. workers. But the movement to the United States of foreign companies and their plants simply underscores how erecting barriers to imports is often fools' gold for those who believe that protection will permanently shelter jobs or the profits of employers.

Third, erecting new barriers to imports also has an unseen boomerang effect in depressing exports. This is one of the most important, but least understood, propositions that we discuss in this book. While higher barriers to imports can temporarily improve the trade balance, this improvement would cause the value of the dollar on world exchange markets to rise, undercutting the competitive position of U.S. exports and curtailing job opportunities for Americans in export industries. Moreover, by increasing the costs of inputs (whether imported or domestic) that producers use to generate goods and services, protection further damages the competitive position of U.S. exporters. This is especially true in high-tech industries, where many American firms rely on foreign-made parts or capital equipment. The dangers of protection are further compounded to the extent it provokes retaliation by other countries. In that event, some Americans who work in exporting industries would lose their jobs, both directly and because higher barriers abroad would induce some of our exporting firms to move their plants (and jobs) overseas. In short, protection is not a zero-sum policy for the United States: it is a *negative sum* policy.

Fourth, globaphobia distracts policymakers and voters from implementing policies that would directly address the major causes of the stagnation or deterioration in the wages of less-skilled Americans. *The most significant problem faced by underpaid workers in the United States is not foreign competition. It is the mismatch between the skills that employers increasingly demand and the skills that many young adults bring to the labor market.* For the next generation of workers, the problem can be addressed by improvements in schooling and public and private training. The more difficult challenge is faced by today's unskilled adults, who find themselves unable to respond to the help wanted ads in daily newspapers, which often call for highly technical skills. It is easy to blame foreign imports for low wages, but doing so will not equip these workers with the new skills that employers need. The role of government is to help those who want to help themselves; most important, by maintaining a high-pressure economy that continues to generate new jobs, and secondarily, by facilitating training and providing effective inducements to displaced workers to find new jobs as rapidly as possible.

Fifth, Americans in fact have a vested interest in negotiating additional reductions of overseas barriers that limit the market for U.S. goods and services. These barriers typically harm the very industries in which America leads the world, including agriculture, financial services, pharmaceuticals, aircraft, and telecommunications. The failure of Congress to grant the president fast-track negotiating authority sends an odd and perverse message to the rest of the world. The United States, which once led the crusade for trade liberalization, now seems to have lost faith in the benefits of trade. Over time, this loss of faith may give ammunition to opponents of free trade in other countries, not only in resisting further trade liberalization but in imposing new barriers.

Sixth, it cannot be stressed too heavily that open trade benefits consumers. Each barrier to trade raises prices not only on the affected imports but also on the domestically produced goods or services with which they compete. Those who would nonetheless have the United States erect barriers to foreign goods—whether in the name of "fair trade," "national security," or some other claimed objective—must face the fact that they are asking the government to tax consumers in order to achieve these goals. And Americans must decide how willing they are to pay that tax. By contrast, lowering barriers to foreign goods delivers the equivalent of a tax cut to American consumers, while encouraging U.S. firms to innovate. The net result is higher living standards for Americans at home.

Finally, to ensure support for free trade, political leaders must abandon the argument traditionally used to advance the cause of trade liberalization: that it will generate *more* jobs. Proponents of freer trade should instead stick with the truth. Total employment depends on the overall macroeconomic environment (the willingness and capacity of Americans to buy goods and services) not on the trade balance (which depends on the difference between the amounts that Americans save and invest). We trade with foreigners for the same reasons that we trade among ourselves: to get better deals. Lower trade barriers in other countries mean *better* jobs for Americans. Firms in industries that are major exporters pay anywhere from 5 to 15 percent more than the average national wage. The "price" for gaining those trade opportunities—reducing our own trade barriers—is one that Americans should be glad to pay.

In spite of the enormous benefits of openness to trade and capital flows from the rest of the world and notwithstanding the additional benefits that Americans would derive from further liberalization, it is important to recognize that open borders create losers as well as winners. Openness exposes workers and company owners to the risk of major losses when new foreign competitors enter the U.S. market. Workers can lose their jobs. This has certainly occurred in a wide range of industries exposed to intense foreign competition—autos, steel, textiles, apparel, and footwear. Indeed, the whole point of engaging in trade is to shift resources—capital and labor—toward their most productive uses, a process that inevitably causes pain to those required to shift. In some cases, workers are forced to accept permanent reductions in pay, either in the jobs they continue to hold in a trade-affected industry or in new jobs they must take after suffering displacement. Other workers, including mainly the unskilled and semiskilled, may be forced to accept small pay reductions as an indirect effect of liberalization. Indeed, the job losses of thousands of similar workers in traded goods industries may tend to push down the wages of *all* workers—even those in the service sector—in a particular skill category.

We acknowledge that these losses occur, though their size is vastly exaggerated in media accounts and the popular imagination. Nonetheless, we believe the nation has both a political and a moral responsibility to offer better compensation to the workers who suffer sizable losses as a result of trade liberalization. In the final chapter we spell out a detailed program for doing so. Decent compensation for the workers who suffer losses is easily affordable in view of the substantial benefits the country enjoys as a result of open trade. Liberal trade, like technological progress, mainly creates winners, not losers. Among the big winners are the stockholders, executives, and workers of exporting firms such as Boeing, Microsoft, and General Electric, as well as Hollywood (whose movies and television shows are seen around the world). There are many millions of more modest winners as well, including the workers, retirees, and nonworking poor, who benefit from lower prices and a far wider and better selection of products.

One problem in making the case for open borders is that few of the winners recognize the extent of the gains they enjoy as a result of free trade. The losses suffered by displaced workers in the auto, apparel, or shoemaking industries are vividly portrayed on the nightly news, but few Americans realize that cars, clothes, and shoes are cheaper, better made, or more varied as a result of their country's openness to the rest of the world. Workers who make products sold outside the United States often fail to recognize how much their jobs and wages depend on America's willingness to import as well as its capacity to export. People contributing to a pension fund seldom realize that their returns (and future pensions) are boosted by the fund's ability to invest overseas, and almost no borrower understands that the cost of a mortgage or car loan is lower because of America's attractiveness to foreigners as a place to invest their money. All of these benefits help improve the standard of living of typical Americans, and they can be directly or indirectly traced to our openness. They are nearly invisible to most citizens, however; certainly far less visible than the painful losses suffered by workers who lose their jobs when a factory is shut down.

To those who believe that reading a book about economics is equivalent to swallowing castor oil, we counsel patience. We will try to change your mind. The economic propositions we discuss are little more than dressed-up common sense. Add some facts, illustrated with a few pictures along the way, and the basic messages of this book can and should be widely accessible to a broad audience.

We begin, in the next chapter, by outlining the case for the policy of openness to foreign goods and services, capital, and to a lesser degree people (immigrants) that the United States has pursued since the end of World War II. The United States has also persuaded an expanding circle of countries to adopt similar policies. Indeed, American success in the cold war was achieved, in part, by trading with other nations and in the process convincing them of the virtues of free markets (domestic and international).

It is therefore ironic that having won the war of ideas by preaching the benefits of openness, the United States now finds itself with a domestic debate over the wisdom of maintaining that policy in the future. In the following chapters of the book, we outline and rebut each of the major challenges mounted by modern critics of globalization: that it has cost Americans jobs and has suppressed average wages; that U.S. firms and workers compete on a playing field tilted by the lax environmental and labor standards of other countries; and that the World Trade Organization, created recently to deal with trade disputes between countries, in fact robs the United States of sovereignty.

The last chapter offers a strategy for making the domestic political environment more amenable to trade liberalization. We outline policies to address the real structural problems that critics of globalization identify but that cannot be ameliorated by the policies they advance.

We cannot conclude this opening chapter without commenting briefly on the economic and political environment in which this book has been written. We started work on the book before the Congressional debate over the extension of fast-track negotiating authority began, convinced that there was a need to help educate the broader public and the policy community about the true implications of globalization—whether or not fast-track was actually approved. As it turned out, fast-track died in the House at the end of 1997 and, at this writing, the prospects for its resurrection in 1998 look clouded, at best.

One of the major complications for those advocating approval of fast-track authority is that since the end of 1997, the economic crisis in Southeast Asia, which began during the summer of that year, has become noticeably worse—much worse than was anticipated even by the best analysts. At this writing, it is impossible to know when the Asian troubles will end, whether they will spread to other countries, and how all this will affect the United States. We will not take up these questions in this book, in large part because anything we say now would be quickly dated in months, if not weeks.

Our aim instead is to take a longer-term view of the process of globalization, for however deep the Asian problems turn out to be, the trend toward increasing integration among the economies of the world is likely to continue—unless policymakers here and abroad succumb to Globaphobia and take a U-turn by raising barriers to trade and investment. As we hope to show in the pages that follow, we believe the overwhelming weight of the evidence suggests that attempts to reverse the tide toward increasing globalization would harm the interests of the great majority of people in the United States and elsewhere around the world.

CHAPTER

2 THE VIRTUES OF OPENNESS

or the past half-century, much as during the country's first decades, the United States has been one of the world's most open economies—and the richest. This connection between wealth and openness is no accident. Americans have invested wisely in businesses and infrastructure for generations. They have been blessed with abundant natural resources. As a group, the people of the United States are well educated and hard-working. But the U.S. economy has also grown faster than others because it has been linked with the rest of the world through trade in goods and services, cross-border flows of investment and saving, and even, to some extent, the movement of people.

The domestic economy of the United States offers vivid proof of the virtues of openness. Consider for a moment how the U.S. economy would operate if each of the fifty states restricted, in one way or another, the movement of goods, services, capital, or labor across its borders. Such impediments might have arisen if the Constitution had not prohibited interstate trade restrictions under its commerce clause. Can anyone plausibly argue that the typical American would be better off in the presence of such restrictions? Would New Yorkers benefit from import duties on goods produced in New Jersey? Would Iowans gain from restrictions on the movement of investment capital from Minnesota or Missouri? Would the residents of Detroit have been better off if they had not been able to move to Texas and California during the 1980s, when U.S. automobile companies reduced their payrolls? The answers to these questions are obvious. The *United* States is clearly a better place to live and work in because impediments to interstate commerce are prohibited by the Constitution.

This is not to suggest that the two hundred or so nations of the world should surrender their sovereignty and embrace world government. That is not only unrealistic, but undesirable. There is intrinsic value in the preservation of a nation's heritage and a world that fosters diversity of cultures and systems of government. But there are also substantial benefits for the people of all nations, including the United States, from the removal of barriers to international commerce.

Facts about Trade

Before outlining the benefits of openness, it is useful briefly to survey a few background facts about U.S. trade. In the process, we try to clear up some of the misunderstandings that have grown up about patterns of trade.

For example, one common myth about U.S. trade is that while the United States primarily imports consumer goods and automobiles, it mainly exports agricultural products and raw materials. Put another way, it is sometimes claimed that the U.S. economy has been so "hollowed out" that Americans must exchange "low value" goods for "higher value" goods made elsewhere.

The facts show otherwise. Figure 2-1 illustrates that in 1996, automobiles and consumer goods together accounted for less than 40 percent of U.S. imports. Capital goods and industrial supplies combined—or the raw materials used to make other goods here—actually made up a larger share, nearly 46 percent. Food and oil took up the balance, about 17 percent.

Figure 2-2, meanwhile, dispels the view that Americans primarily export food and raw materials. These exports are important, to be sure, accounting together for about one-third of the total. But capital goods—machines and other sophisticated equipment— account for a larger share of the total, over 41 percent. And con-

Figure 2-1. Composition of U.S. Goods Imports, 1996

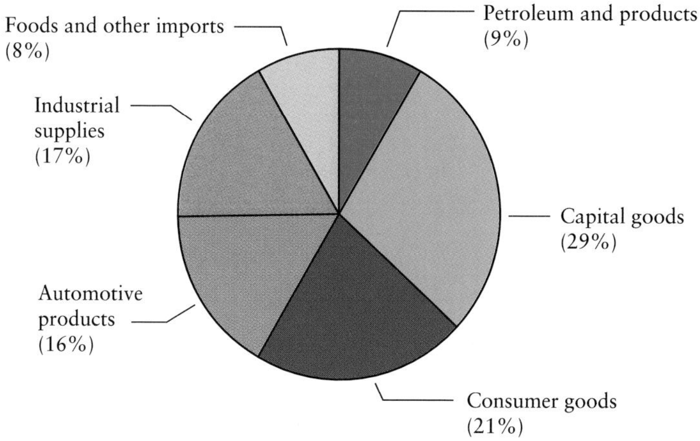

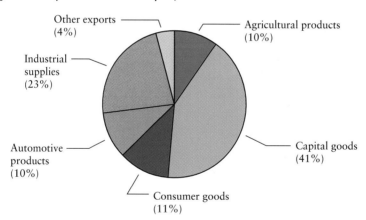

Foods and other imports — (8%)

Petroleum and products (9%)

Industrial supplies (17%)

Capital goods (29%)

Automotive products (16%)

Consumer goods (21%)

Source: Federal Reserve Bank at Washington (1997).

Figure 2-2. Composition of U.S. Goods Exports, 1996

Other exports (4%)

Agricultural products (10%)

Industrial supplies (23%)

Automotive products (10%)

Capital goods (41%)

Consumer goods (11%)

Source: Federal Reserve Bank at Washington (1997).

sumer goods and automotive products together account for almost 22 percent.

Other myths surround the places where the United States imports goods from and sends them to. Judging from the preponderance of newspaper stories about imports, Americans could be excused for believing that most U.S. imports come from Japan and Mexico. Figure

Figure 2-3. Sources of U.S. Goods Imports, 1996

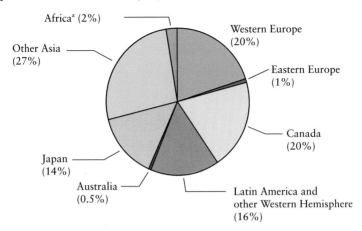

Source: *Survey of Current Business*, October 1997.
a. Excluding South Africa.

2-3 shows, however, that Japan and all of Latin American combined contribute only 30 percent of U.S. imports. Canada and western Europe send about 40 percent, and the rest of the world takes up the balance. Figure 2-4 presents a roughly similar pattern for U.S. exports. Again, in light of all the press accounts of trade barriers in Japan, in particular, it may be surprising to realize that nearly 11 percent of U.S. exports go to that country, a slightly lower share than the Japanese share of U.S. imports, to be sure, but comparable.

Goods are only part of what the United States sends across its borders. An increasingly important component of U.S. trade involves *services*—a catch-all category that includes everything traded that is not tangible. As shown in figure 2-5, even as the United States has experienced a continuing deficit in goods trade, it has enjoyed a steadily widening *surplus* in services trade. Whether and how seriously one should take all these figures about the U.S. balance of trade are important questions; we address them later in this chapter and again in chapter 4.

Of what does services trade actually consist? Figure 2-6 shows that about half of the imports of services represent travel that Americans undertake abroad. At first blush, this appears contradictory: when Americans go overseas, do we not export travel? Actually, it is the other way other around. When American travel elsewhere, they are

Figure 2-4. Destinations of U.S. Goods Exports, 1996

Africaᵃ (2%)

Other Asia (22%)

Western Europe (22%)

Eastern Europe (1%)

Japan (11%)

Australia (2%)

Canada (22%)

Latin America and other Western Hemisphere (18%)

Source: *Survey of Current Business*, October 1997.
a. Excluding South Africa.

purchasing travel services there, and thus importing them here. Correspondingly, travel by foreigners here represents a leading U.S. export, as shown in figure 2-7. Other important services exports include insurance and financial services, royalties and license fees, and transportation.

Figure 2-5. Net Trade in Goods and in Services as Shares of U.S. GDP, 1960–96
Percent of GDP

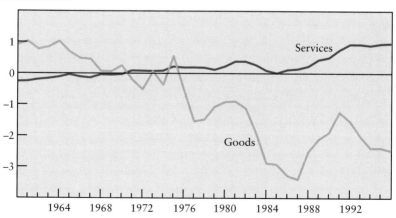

Services

Goods

1964   1968   1972   1976   1980   1984   1988   1992

Source: Council of Economic Advisers (1997).

Figure 2-6. Composition of U.S. Private Services Imports, 1996

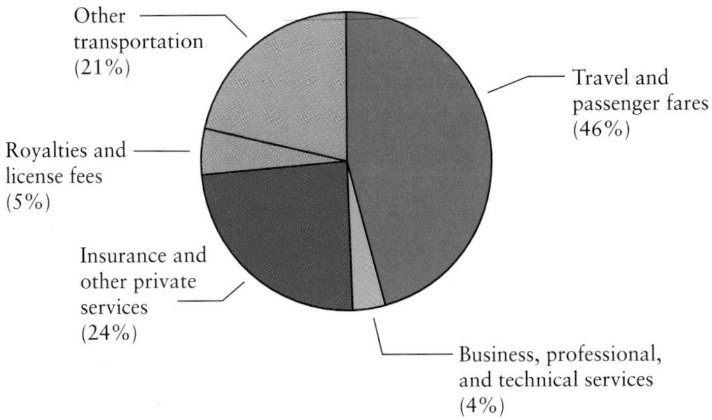

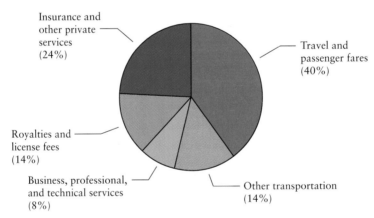

Other transportation (21%)

Travel and passenger fares (46%)

Royalties and license fees (5%)

Insurance and other private services (24%)

Business, professional, and technical services (4%)

Source: Federal Reserve Bank at Washington (1997).

Figure 2-7. Composition of U.S. Private Services Exports, 1996

Insurance and other private services (24%)

Travel and passenger fares (40%)

Royalties and license fees (14%)

Business, professional, and technical services (8%)

Other transportation (14%)

Source: Federal Reserve Bank at Washington (1997).

Benefits of Trade

Since publication of Adam Smith's pathbreaking *Wealth of Nations*—in 1776, the same year as the American Declaration of Independence—economists have agreed on the proposition that people, companies, and nations should trade with one another to enhance their standard of living. There are at least four broad reasons why this is so.

Trade and Efficient Production

Most people, whether they realize it or not, are familiar with the advantages of trade at a purely personal level. Workers "export" their services to employers, and then use the money that they earn to "import" food, clothing, housing, education, and medical care. This exchange of labor for goods and services produced by others is sensible because it is *more efficient to specialize and trade.* We work in jobs where our skills make us particularly valuable, and we let others process our food, manufacture our clothing, and educate our children. The mutual benefit of trade was one of Adam Smith's central insights. Specialization and trade allow entire economies to produce far more goods and services than would be the case if individuals had to produce everything for themselves.

David Ricardo, another famous British economist, refined and extended Smith's insight about the virtues of specialization in his principle of "comparative advantage." Ricardo demonstrated that even if a nation were better than other countries at producing everything, that nation would still be better off if it concentrated on producing the things that it was comparatively best at producing and traded for the rest.

How nations come to be "best" at producing particular things depends not just on their natural endowments, such as the amount of land or natural resources they may be lucky (or unlucky) to possess, but also on a variety of factors that may be historical accidents but nonetheless can have powerful effects on trade patterns and benefits for consumers. For example, as a result of the accumulation of high-technology firms in Silicon Valley (spawned in large part by forward-thinking talent at academic centers like Berkeley and Stanford universities) or the growth of the fashion industry in northern Italy, firms or groups of firms that locate in these regions gain powerful advantages simply from being able to tap into a common pool of labor, talent, and ideas—from being "close to the action." Free trade can and does promote these newer sources of comparative advantage, which economists have labeled, in their technical jargon, "economies of agglomeration."

The principle of comparative advantage is easy to illustrate using two famous sports personalities. Because there are only a fixed number of waking hours in which he can work, Tiger Woods clearly profits from devoting his time to practicing and playing golf. He would be foolish to try to make his own golf clubs. Woods maximizes his income by perfecting his golf game, while those who specialize in making golf clubs maximize theirs. Both parties are better off than they would be without trade, *even if Woods could make splendid golf clubs himself.* In a recent college economics textbook, Gregory Mankiw makes the same point by suggesting that it makes no economic sense for Michael Jordan to mow his own lawn when he could be improving his dunks and jump shots.[1] What is true for Tiger Woods and Michael Jordan is true for everyone else, and for countries as well. Each should devote its scarce time and resources to producing the goods and services that it is best at producing.

The principle of comparative advantage has two important, and often ignored, implications. *First, it necessarily implies that nations export in order to import.* By definition, if nations specialize in what they are comparatively best at producing, they must import goods and services that other countries produce best. The notion that imports are "bad" while exports are "good"—popular in the media and among politicians—is long overdue for correction.

Second, trade is not a zero-sum game, in which one nation wins only at the expense of its competitors. Just as workers are mutually better off trading their labor for the consumer goods and services produced by others, nations are mutually better off when firms and workers produce and trade the goods and services in which they enjoy a comparative advantage in exchange for goods and services that they can purchase more cheaply from others.

Trade and Efficient Consumption

The corollary to the proposition that trade makes overall production more efficient is that it makes goods and services cheaper for consumers. As consumers, we are all better off if we can purchase food, clothing, and shelter at lower cost than if we had to produce each of these items ourselves. In this way, trade raises the purchasing power of the incomes that we earn from work.

Consumers benefit from trade not only because imported goods can be (and often are) cheaper than their domestically produced counter-

1. Mankiw (1997, p. 53).

Figure 2-8. Changes in Prices of Traded Goods Relative to Other Goods and Services, 1980–96

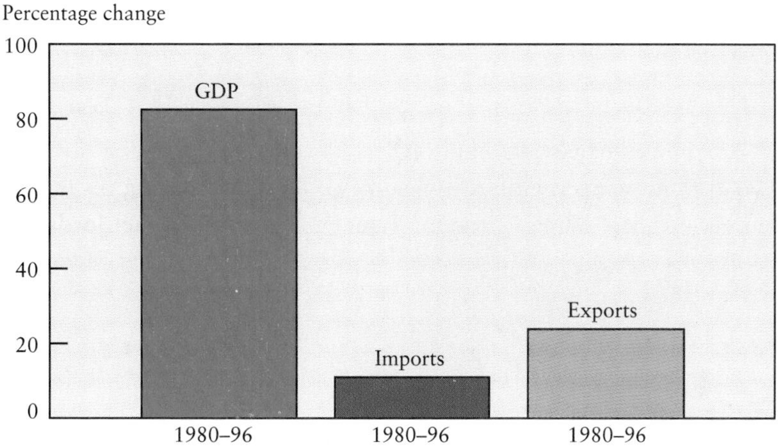

Percentage change

Source: Council of Economic Advisers (1997).

parts, but also because the competition provided by imports, or the mere threat of imports, keeps domestic producers from charging excessive prices. In addition, competition from imports encourages them to innovate and produce better products and services at lower cost. Similarly, the hot breath of foreign competition helps to sharpen the competitive edge of domestic industries engaged in exporting. Figure 2-8 shows that prices of both imports and exports in fact have increased far less rapidly since 1980 than have prices throughout the economy as a whole.

Some critics of globalization see its dampening effect on prices as a disadvantage, pointing to the threat of a "global glut" of goods from the less developed world as a source of deflationary pressure. Yet as we explain in chapter 4, imports from the developing countries represent only about 4 percent of total U.S. output, and thus can have only a marginal impact on both output and the overall rate of price inflation in the United States. Even so, by helping to restrain inflation, competition from elsewhere around the world—as tough as it may be—allows the Federal Reserve to tolerate somewhat faster overall growth and lower rates of unemployment than might otherwise be the case. Indeed, as painful as the economic crisis in Asia has been for the residents in that part of the world, the slowdown in U.S. exports that the trauma inevitably will cause already has delayed a boost in interest

Figure 2-9. Annual Percentage Growth Rates of GDP and Trade, World and United States, 1959 to mid-1990s

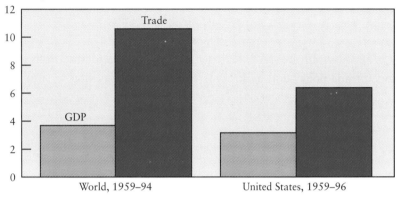

Source: GATT (1984/85, 1995).

rates that many believed the Federal Reserve otherwise would have implemented to cool off the rapid growth of the economy. And if the Asian crisis grows worse, the Fed may even lower interest rates to keep unemployment from rising.

The gains to consumers afforded by the postwar liberalization of trade help to explain why the volume of world trade has expanded at a much faster pace than world output, as is shown in figure 2-9. Likewise, the growth of U.S. trade has substantially outpaced the growth of U.S. output. Tariff reductions around the world, the result of large multilateral trade deals, have been instrumental in bringing this about. But the fact that trade allows firms and workers to specialize in what they do best restrains the prices of internationally traded products, encouraging consumers to increase their purchases of these at a faster pace than their consumption of other goods and services.

Moreover, freer trade not only lowers prices, it also enhances product variety. No country has a monopoly in the production of quality goods. Americans have benefited from importing fax machines and video cassette recorders, among other items, that are overwhelmingly or exclusively made abroad. By the same token, consumers in other countries enjoy a broad range of computer software and hardware that is produced only in the United States.

Trade and Competition

By now it should be clear that, for consumers, there is no fundamental difference between trade and competition that takes place across borders and within borders. This general principle underlies both U.S. open trade policy and antitrust laws: competition is vital to ensuring that firms have an incentive to produce goods and services at the lowest cost. And it makes no distinction between domestic and foreign competition. In fact, foreign firms can help to supply competition that may be weak at home, and thereby help to deliver the benefits of lower prices that U.S. antitrust laws promise.

At this point, critics of free trade may object that foreign competition is different, because firms abroad do not play by the same rules that American firms must respect. Foreign competition is thus "unfair." The harshest complaints about unfair practices are often lodged against firms in countries where wages are much lower than in the United States. We address these objections in chapters 4 and 5.

Trade and Innovation

The efficiency benefits of trade described so far are "static." That is, they refer to the gains that producers and consumers realize from trade assuming the production methods and products of each country do not change. Economies, however, are dynamic. Production methods and consumer products are constantly being changed and improved. Analysts who study economic growth have established that, directly or indirectly, as much as half of U.S. economic growth can be traced to economic innovation: new products and production processes; new ways of financing, marketing, and distributing goods; and new strategies for managing businesses and organizing employment.

Open trade promotes economic innovation in several ways: by spurring product competition among companies in the same line of business, by exposing domestic firms to the best new ideas from around the world, and by enabling these firms to import high-technology capital equipment and know-how, so that they can manufacture products and deliver services at lower costs than if they were restricted to buying domestically produced inputs. For proof, one need only look at the U.S. automobile industry, which in the early 1970s had grown complacent, but in the face of stiff Japanese competition has since become more efficient and improved the quality (and thus the value) of its products.

Traditional Qualifications to Free Trade

Even Adam Smith was willing to make one exception to his endorsement of free trade: protection can be justified for domestic industries that are vital to a nation's defense. Common sense suggests that countries should not rely on foreigners of uncertain future allegiance to produce specialized military equipment. National security arguments have also been extended to cover trade in certain commodities, such as oil, that are essential to the armed forces in time of war.

Interestingly, since World War II the national security argument has been advanced more frequently in the cause of trade *liberalization* than that of protection of the United States. Open trade became an important component of the American policy of promoting capitalism and democracy as a shield against communism. Now that communism has disappeared in much of the world, national security arguments have become less important in the debate over trade.

Alexander Hamilton, in the late eighteenth century, offered a second qualification to liberal trade in his classic *Report on Manufactures*: If an underdeveloped economy like newly independent America were to achieve a prominent place in the world, it would have to develop the manufacturing capacity of an advanced country.[2] That goal might be achieved by imposing temporary tariffs on the manufactured products of more advanced countries. However, once the "infant" domestic industries were established, Hamilton argued, the ingenuity of Americans would ensure that we could produce the goods more cheaply than foreigners, and the trade protection could safely end.

This argument gained much broader support when first the Whigs and then the new Republican party adopted it as part of the call for a new American nationalism. For Hamilton—as later for Henry Clay,

2. U.S. Department of the Treasury (1892).

Abraham Lincoln, and Theodore Roosevelt—protection for infant industries was part of a broader case for a strong central government, powerful enough to promote strategically the nation's long-term economic interest and development. In this view, high tariffs were a just fee charged to foreign countries for the privilege of selling in American markets, and free trade was a kind of malignancy, carrying corrupt foreign values. Nor did it escape the attention of politicians that tariffs and duties could finance the federal government without imposing the direct taxes then barred by the Constitution.

This tide of nationalistic protectionism was bolstered by the economic conditions and ideas of the time. Most nineteenth-century economists continued to follow Adam Smith's logic, that a nation will produce less wealth under protection than under free trade. But theories propounded in the 1840s by the Austrian Friedrich List, who argued that tariffs could produce long-term benefits by protecting fledgling manufacturers until these accumulated the expertise to compete with more well-established foreign firms, gathered political currency. The nineteenth-century British philosopher John Stuart Mill, while calling protection in general "an organized system of pillage of the many by the few," defended selected tariffs "if they are imposed temporarily (especially in a young and rising nation) in hopes of naturalizing a foreign industry, in itself perfectly suitable to the circumstances of the country."[3]

Today, however, infant industry arguments are hard to take seriously in the United States. The economy is no longer a stepchild of Great Britain, but the most efficient, productive, and innovative in the world. The dynamic U.S. economy is constantly developing new products and services—each of which becomes, as it were, an "infant industry." Should the government get into the business of deciding if any of these actual or potential industries promise sufficiently broad social benefits (exceeding any benefits that may be reaped by private investors) that they deserve some kind of public aid or protection? To answer yes requires a remarkable degree of faith—first, in the government's ability to identify which industries will or should survive after the initial period of "temporary" protection has passed; and second, in its will-

3. Mill (1909, p. 922); Elliot (1910, vol. 2, p. 295).

ingness to do so in an objective, nonpolitical manner, especially given that protection suspends the market competition that normally sorts out winners from losers.

The record on this score is hardly encouraging. In the 1970s, for example, French and English aircraft manufacturers won large government subsidies to develop the Concorde and claim the market for supersonic commercial aircraft. The Concorde won that battle, but lost vast sums of taxpayers' money in the process; the project never turned a profit. More recently, Japanese and European governments tried, unsuccessfully and wastefully, to pick technologies for high definition television, while the United States left its development to the market. It is the unprotected American firms that now appear poised to achieve commercial success and to set the technological standard for the world market. In broader terms, the Japanese were, for a while, successful in creating some world-class industries with some degree of government help (targeted credit, in particular) and protection. But in the process many other industries (such as retailing) were left behind and have suffered subnormal productivity.[4]

In short, the exceptions to arguments for free trade traditionally recognized by economists and by a long line of politicians have little relevance for most U.S. industries. As a result, modern critics rest their cases on other, much broader, arguments that lead to even more sweeping indictments of greater openness. We outline these claims at the end of this chapter and examine the evidence behind them throughout the rest of the book.

Trade and Disruption

Any discussion of the benefits of freer trade is incomplete without recognition that not everyone wins with more open trade. The introduction of new technologies that make life easier and richer usually will hurt some established producers. And, on a far smaller scale, so does trade liberalization. Firms and workers who make goods or services that are displaced by imports suffer at least temporary losses as a result of lower trade barriers. But no one would suggest halting tech-

4. See Baily (1993).

nological progress because it adversely affects workers who make out-dated products. And one should not turn away from the liberalization of trade for essentially identical reasons. Rather, one can and should do what is needed to help the workers and firms that are affected adversely by freer trade to find a prosperous niche in the richer economy. The challenge is to extend and expand open markets while providing everyone access to the education and skills needed to prosper in them. In our concluding chapter, we provide suggestions for meeting that challenge.

Benefiting from the Free Trade of Others

We have stressed the benefits of free trade to any country that opens its borders to goods and services from outside. Indeed, most American economists believe that these benefits are so large that a country should practice *unilateral* free trade, regardless of the trade barriers erected by other countries. As economist Frederic Bastiat noted in the nineteenth century, it makes no more sense to erect trade barriers because other countries have them than it would to block up one's own harbors because other countries have rocky coastlines. Farsighted policymakers in the United States and abroad have acted on the basis of Bastiat's insight.

President Woodrow Wilson was an early proponent of unilateral trade liberalization. He took advantage of authority given him by Congress to cut tariffs and keep them low through World War I. Wilson's trade policies were reversed by President William Harding, however, who used the power granted by the postwar Republican Congress to raise tariffs against any nation that discriminated against U.S. exports. After the end of World War II, Presidents Truman and Eisenhower once again cut U.S. tariffs, to facilitate the economic recovery of the European allies and anchor the defeated Axis countries to the noncommunist West. Eisenhower—and, later, President Kennedy—also cut tariffs on imports from third world countries and some other small countries, hoping to spur their economies and thus to build bulwarks against communism. Much more recently, the economic damage experienced by those Latin American countries that during the 1960s and 1970s followed the "import substitution" model of economic development—a policy resting on the infant industry argument and thus inherently protectionist—has led a number of developing countries to recognize the benefits of liberalization.

It is rare for an American politician today to champion the cause of unilateral free trade. To do so exposes elected officials to the charge of "unilateral disarmament." After all, the United States would not abandon all its weapons, leaving it open to attack from other countries. Why should this country surrender trade barriers and expose domestic firms to intensified import competition without obtaining improved opportunities for exporting companies? We lay out some detailed answers to this question in chapter 5. For now, we provide a brief preview.

While it may be in a nation's interest to drop its own trade barriers unilaterally—much as Hong Kong has done, with extraordinary success—that nation can be even better off if the promise of such reductions induces other nations to drop or lower their barriers as well. This is the reasoning behind the commonsense notion of "reciprocity," an idea that helped to undo the enormous damage that the infamous Hawley-Smoot Tariff Act of 1930 inflicted on U.S. trade and economic activity around the world. In 1934 Congress gave President Franklin Roosevelt the authority to negotiate reciprocal tariff reductions of up to 50 percent with other countries, without having to obtain further congressional approval.[5] Roosevelt used this authority to complete thirty-two bilateral trade agreements by 1945.

By definition, however, bilateral trade agreements are of limited effect. They encourage trade only between the two countries involved. Indeed, bilateral trade pacts can even lead to some inefficiency, by diverting trade flows away from countries that may be more efficient in producing the traded goods and services than producers located in the two countries that participate in the deal. As the number of bilateral arrangements multiply, trade can become balkanized and distorted. Bureaucrats must administer complicated "rules of origin" to

---

5. The 1934 act also reduced the leverage of domestic industries that sought protection, by shifting the coordination and supervision of trade negotiations to the new semisecret executive branch Committee on Trade Agreements, composed of technical experts.

determine which imports are eligible for the special treatment that the various deals promise.

After World War II, the United States recognized these difficulties and persuaded other countries to adopt a wholly new trade arrangement, based on the principles of "multilateral reciprocity" and most favored nation (MFN) treatment. These were embodied in the General Agreement on Tariffs and Trade (GATT). By grouping together many different types of liberalization at the same time, multilateral trade deals can generate enough benefits for the parties involved to more than offset the costs to those sectors facing tougher competition when protection is eased. MFN treatment simply means that each party to a trade deal agrees not to discriminate in favor of or against any other party, so that all signatory countries get the benefit of the lowest barriers that have been negotiated. The MFN principle greatly enlarges the benefits of belonging to the group of nations that have committed themselves to abide by it.

GATT is one of the most successful innovations in the history of international relations. Over the past fifty years, its member countries have negotiated eight major "rounds" of reductions in trade barriers. During this period, average tariffs in industrialized countries have plummeted from over 40 percent to just 6 percent. As tariffs have been lowered, however, other nontariff barriers to trade have become more visible, and thus have become targets for negotiation. The most recent GATT arrangement—the Uruguay Round, completed in 1994—is probably the most comprehensive trade deal in world history. Signed by a record 125 countries, the Uruguay agreement commits parties to reduce remaining tariffs by an average of nearly 40 percent and to phase out over ten years long-standing worldwide quotas on textile and apparel exports. It is also the first such agreement to cover trade-related intellectual property rights, bring agricultural trade under GATT discipline, outlaw voluntary export restraints, and restrain both domestic subsidies for export industries and antidumping duties on foreign imports, and it places trade in services on GATT's agenda for the future. Perhaps most significant for the long run, the Uruguay agreement created the World Trade Organization, to improve the process of settling international disputes, a move that has attracted much criticism that, for reasons that we outline later in the book, is unfounded.

Liberalized trade has been good for consumers in the United States and elsewhere. The World Bank expects consumers to gain between $100 billion and $200 billion *every year* in additional purchasing power as a result of the Uruguay agreement, with two-thirds going to rich countries, including the United States.[6] Large benefits should also flow to consumers from the landmark agreement reached in late 1997 between the United States and many of its trading partners to remove tariffs on high-technology products, as well as from implementation of the agreement reached in early 1997, under the auspices of the WTO, to liberalize telecommunications markets around the world.[7] Likewise, the recently completed WTO agreement on financial services—under which several other countries, especially in the developing world, will drop many of their barriers blocking entry by foreign financial services providers—should prove to be greatly beneficial to U.S. financial services companies, which are among the leaders in the field. Financial services rank as a major American service export; assuming the commitments under the WTO agreement are fulfilled, the financial services share of the services export pie should only grow in the future.

Some critics of the postwar consensus in favor of freer trade have charged that the United States has received the short end of the stick, having been forced to open its economy to a greater degree than other countries. Clearly, the U.S. economy is more open than many others, and has been so for the past fifty years. But the changes in trade barriers resulting from past trade deals have also tilted strongly in our favor. Under the Uruguay Round agreement, for example, the United States will lower its tariffs by about 2 percentage points, while other nations must chop theirs between 3 and 8 percent. Likewise, under the North American Free Trade Agreement (NAFTA)—which we discuss more extensively in the next chapter—Mexico has pledged to eliminate its tariffs on U.S. products, which averaged about 10 percent before the

6. World Bank (1995, p. 57).
7. Schott (1996).

agreement, while the United States agreed to eliminate the 4 percent duties previously levied on Mexican exports.

In spite of the benefits they have conferred, large multilateral trade negotiations have fallen out of political favor since the Uruguay Round. The length of that negotiation, which took more than a decade to complete, and the difficulties that nations have faced in grappling with many of the remaining nontariff barriers help to explain why policymakers have become disenchanted with multilateral bargaining. Instead, the United States and other countries have increasingly turned to regional trade deals, which are permitted under article 24 of GATT, so long as the arrangements drop "substantially all" barriers among the members and do not raise barriers to nonmember countries. Since the early 1980s, the United States has concluded free trade agreements with Israel, Canada, and Mexico. And in the Mercosur trade arrangement, six South American countries are endeavoring to copy the European Union, a much broader and well-developed regional arrangement. Since its creation in 1948, GATT has sanctioned over one hundred regional trade arrangements, nearly one-third of which were completed between 1990 and 1994 alone.[8]

As with the proliferation of bilateral trade deals before GATT was created (largely to halt that trend), the growing number of regional arrangements has raised fears among some advocates of global liberalization that trade will increasingly become balkanized and distorted—that the regional deals will become stumbling blocks rather than building blocks for much broader liberalization efforts. It is true that regional deals do not offer as many opportunities for bargaining (trading off various interests against each other) as do large multilateral negotiations. But they can nonetheless prove beneficial if in the process of eliminating barriers within the group, they also lower barriers with respect to outsiders and offer membership to other countries.

The Clinton administration implicitly sought to pursue such a positive approach by asking Congress for fast-track negotiating authority to expand NAFTA to include all nations in the Western Hemisphere, as well as to accomplish a free trade arrangement with the Asia Pacific

8. Frankel (1997).

Economic Cooperation (APEC) forum. The administration's failure to obtain that authority, so far, may send the unfortunate signal that other nations should form regional pacts excluding the United States, as Canada is doing by negotiating with the Mercosur countries. This could lead to the very distortions of trade that some ardent free traders have feared of regional arrangements. Indeed, if fast-track is not authorized, American firms now exporting goods to South America would ironically have an increased incentive to shift production out of the United States into member countries of Mercosur, in order to take advantage of lower trade barriers within that region. As it is, Chile—which was counting on fast-track to pave the way for a bilateral free trade agreement with the United States—has already been shifting its trade to Canada and Mexico.[9]

In any event, trade liberalization remains an unfinished task. Despite all of the progress that has been made in lowering trade barriers, tariffs in many developing countries range up to 30 percent and higher. Agricultural quotas, barriers to foreign services providers, and other investment restrictions translate into tariff-equivalent rates of protection of 50 percent or more. Removing these barriers would speed the growth of low-income but rapidly growing economies, which, in turn, would spur demand for capital goods produced by high-wage industries in the developed world.

Developed countries, too, maintain significant trade barriers in some key sectors. Although the Uruguay Round commendably converted most agricultural quotas into tariffs, tariffs (or the tariff equivalent of quotas) on dairy items and sugar exceed 100 percent in the European Union and stand at nearly 100 percent in the United States; in Japan, dairy tariffs exceed 300 percent and tariffs on wheat remain above 150 percent. New trade negotiations could speed up the transition and thereby reduce prices for consumers more quickly.

The United States, in particular, has much to gain from further reductions of barriers to trade and investment. America has the world's most efficient producers of agricultural commodities and is the leading producer of software, telecommunications, entertainment, and finan-

---

9. After growing by more than 40 percent between 1994 and 1996, total U.S. trade with Chile has since virtually stopped expanding. See Faiola (1997).

cial services. All these industries would benefit from improved access to foreign markets.

Benefits of Cross-Border Investment

Just as trade in commodities between countries is beneficial, so too is trade in assets, or the transfer of savings across national borders. Individuals and institutions in the United States, for example, can improve the performance of their investment portfolios by diversifying more broadly into foreign assets. At the same time, countries that receive these investment flows benefit by having access to cheaper capital than they would if they had to rely solely on domestic savings.

The Inseparable Link between Foreign Trade and Investment

It is important to recognize, at the outset, that foreign trade and investment are linked by fundamental economic factors reflected in national income accounting. By definition, at any point in time a nation's balance on its "current account" (which includes both trade and various overseas transfer payments) must equal the balance on its "capital account" (the net flow of assets into and out of the country). For example, when a country imports more than it exports, the people and firms within it must find ways to obtain the foreign currency needed to purchase the excess foreign imports. They can do this either by selling some of their foreign assets or by borrowing the foreign currency from foreign residents or institutions (by obtaining overseas bank loans, for instance, or by issuing debt or equity). The current account deficit matches the net inflow of capital. This process is reversed when a country runs a current account surplus, which must be matched by a net outflow of capital.

The accounting identity between the current account and capital account is not reflected perfectly in government statistics, which typically show a discrepancy between the two. Nonetheless, the current and capital accounts move roughly in tandem. For example, since the early 1980s, the United States has run large current account deficits, financed with a substantial increase in its net foreign borrowing. As a result, its net asset position relative to the rest of the world—in other words, total U.S. investments abroad minus foreigners' investments in America—turned from a positive (or net creditor) position of $260 billion in 1982 to a negative (or net debtor) position in excess of $700 billion by year end 1996.

In short, any nation that trades with other countries must exchange capital flows with them; and any nation with capital flows across its borders must trade. Nations offering an economic climate that produces healthy returns on investments, as does the United States, attract capital from the rest of the world. As capital flows into a country, its trade balance can deteriorate. But that does not mean that the nation is worse off. On the contrary, if foreign investors are adding to the productive capacity of an economy and perhaps also providing new ideas that improve efficiency, they are helping to make the economy more productive. Therefore the trade and current account balances, taken by themselves, are poor measures of a nation's economic well-being (which we discuss further in chapter 5).

Why It Is Good to Attract Foreign Investment

Foreign investment is usually classified in one of two categories: "portfolio investment," representing purchases by foreigners of stocks, bonds, and other financial assets that can be readily sold on the open market, and "direct investment," which includes purchases by foreign investors of real estate or a sufficient block of stock to provide a meaningful degree of control over a company.[10] When a foreign company buys or builds a facility in the United States, it is counted as direct investment.

Portfolio investment not only finances trade, but adds to the pool of funds available for capital investment by domestic residents, and thereby reduces the domestic interest rate below what it would otherwise be. During the 1980s and much of the 1990s, the United States gained enormously from the willingness of foreign central banks, private firms, and individuals to buy the substantial volumes of new

10. U.S. government statistics count a company as "foreign owned" if as little as 10 percent of its stock is owned by foreign nationals.

Treasury debt that were put on the market each year to finance large federal budget deficits. Had foreigners declined to purchase the debt, interest rates would have been higher in the United States, and accordingly investment in new plant and equipment almost certainly would have been lower.[11]

Like portfolio investment, direct capital flows broaden the pool of funds available for domestic investment and thus reduce the cost of capital to domestic companies. But the benefits of direct investment are potentially even more far-reaching. While the U.S. economy today may be the world's most productive and innovative, it does not have a monopoly on good ideas. Along with their money, foreign direct investors usually bring their ideas about good production practices and new products. Many of these innovations eventually leak out to their domestically owned competitors, and thus to American managers and workers. For example, Japanese manufacturers introduced to America lean production techniques, "just in time" delivery systems and close supplier relationships when they set up their own assembly plants here. Recognizing the benefits of this system, dozens of other American corporations have adopted these techniques. Other management innovations, such as "quality circles" on the shop floor and other quality control techniques (many pioneered by the American Edward Deming, who for many decades was taken more seriously in Japan than here), have been introduced in U.S. firms in the same way. Today, America attracts more foreign direct investment than any other country. About 5 percent of all working Americans are employed in companies owned wholly or in substantial part by foreign investors.

For all the attention that politicians and voters have paid to Japanese investment in the United States, it is still important to realize that Japan nonetheless ranks only as the second most important source of foreign direct investment in the country. As shown in figure 2-10, through 1996 the United Kingdom ranked first and (surprising as it may be to some) the Netherlands ranked third. Other European countries and Canada have also been major sources of foreign direct invest-

---

11. On the other side, had foreigners not been so willing to invest in the United States, the value of the dollar would not have appreciated so much during the first part of the 1980s, and thus Americans exporters would not have suffered such a deep erosion in their international competitive position.

Figure 2-10. Sources of Foreign Direct Investment in the United States, 1996

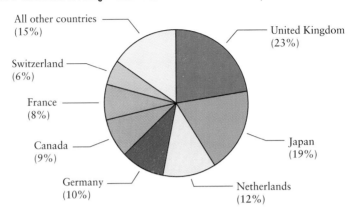

All other countries (15%)

United Kingdom (23%)

Switzerland (6%)

France (8%)

Canada (9%)

Japan (19%)

Germany (10%)

Netherlands (12%)

Source: Quinlan (1997b).

ment. Figure 2-11 shows the U.S. industries in which foreigners invested, as of 1996. Manufacturing ranks first, capturing over a third of the total, with finance, insurance, and banking a relatively close second at a quarter of the total, and a variety of other sectors taking up the balance.

While the globalization of capital flows is unequivocally good for a rich country like the United States, with a well-established credit reputation and, since the thrift and banking debacles of the 1980s, a well-supervised and strongly capitalized financial sector, short-term capital flows can be destabilizing for less developed countries that have neither of these advantages. This has been demonstrated all too clearly in the winter of 1997–98 in Southeast Asia (and earlier, in Mexico), where businesses, banks, and governments unwisely borrowed in foreign currencies in short maturities. This strategy carried the risk that if and when the investors had to be repaid, domestic borrowers could be hard pressed to find scarce foreign exchange. The danger was compounded by lax supervision of financial institutions, which were allowed to embark on ill-fated lending sprees to support unproductive investments, financed by foolhardy foreign investors who were too eager to part with their money for only slightly higher returns than they could earn at home. When the financial "bubbles" burst, domestic and for-

Figure 2-11. Composition of Foreign Direct Investment in the United States, 1996

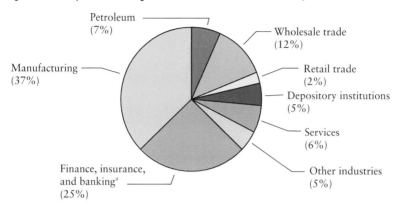

Petroleum
(7%)

Wholesale trade
(12%)

Manufacturing
(37%)

Retail trade
(2%)

Depository institutions
(5%)

Services
(6%)

Finance, insurance,
and banking[a]
(25%)

Other industries
(5%)

Source: Data are from the Bureau of Economic Analysis, accessed on the bureau's worldwide web page.
a. Finance does not include banking.

eign investors took their money out of the domestic currencies, sending the values of those currencies into tailspins.

The leaders of some developing countries have been tempted by their sudden falls from grace to restrict capital flows, both to prevent their currencies from becoming overvalued in the first place and to avoid the currency crises that subsequently occur when investors rush to sell those currencies all at once. Countries that discourage short-term capital flows, however, also run the risk of discouraging long-term foreign direct investment, which may be even more valuable to them than is foreign direct investment to the United States. If potential long-term investors face the risk of not being able to withdraw future earnings and dividends, they may be discouraged from making any investment in these countries in the first place.

Fortunately, there are better solutions. One is to strengthen supervision of financial institutions and enforce sound capital standards, both in order to discourage banks from engaging in excessive lending and to reinforce their financial positions, so that they can withstand loan losses should they occur.[12] The International Monetary Fund is making these steps a principal condition for extending credit to the nations of

12. For a thorough guide to appropriate banking reforms, see Goldstein (1997).

Southeast Asia. A second productive step would be to discourage local businesses and financial institutions from borrowing too heavily in foreign currencies, especially on a short-term basis. A third step would be to make the financial positions of banks, other financial institutions, and firms in general more transparent, so that investors—domestic and foreign alike—are better able to assess the balance sheets of these companies. If there is anything that contributes to panic, it is the lack of sufficient, accurate, and timely information.

Specific Benefits of U.S. Investment Abroad

The growth and prosperity of the U.S. economy also depend on American capital seeking profitable investment opportunities outside the United States. Portfolio investment in overseas companies offers one route to good financial rewards. A basic tenet of modern finance theory is that investors can obtain higher returns for given levels of risk (or equivalently, the same returns for lower levels of risk) by diversifying their investments broadly across firms and industries. The same logic applies to the diversification of investments across countries. The economic fortunes of different countries are, to some extent, independent. Investors can offset the weak performance of one market by being invested in many others. Although American investors are a long way from fully diversifying their holdings of securities to conform with the best financial advice, a growing percentage of investors does recognize the benefits of cross-country diversification. In 1975 only 1 percent of equities held by American investors were in foreign stocks. By 1996 that share had risen to 10 percent.[13]

Outward foreign direct investment provides potentially more far-reaching benefits. Once, the world was dominated by trade in commodities, which, after their manufacture, simply required transportation to foreign destinations. Today, however, much U.S. trade requires a significant presence by American firms in foreign countries; otherwise it would not occur, to the detriment of U.S. workers in export industries. Many American-made products require sales and customer support services abroad. And many services exported by U.S. firms,

13. Werner and Tesar (1998).

especially by financial, legal, and consulting businesses, are largely delivered in person, through foreign offices. Moreover, local research and development facilities enable multinational firms to tailor products and services to foreign markets and learn about ideas that are developed abroad. By investing overseas, Americans firms are in a vastly better position to gain the local knowledge that they need in order to tap into markets around the world.

Just as actual or threatened trade restrictions in the United States have induced manufacturers from Japan and elsewhere to invest in this country, foreign trade barriers have led American companies to invest abroad. Automobile workers in Detroit now produce parts that are shipped to American-owned assembly plants in other countries to serve foreign automobile buyers around the world, from Spain to Thailand. And how secure would be the jobs of Kodak workers in Rochester, New York, if their company could not invest and expand its operations elsewhere around the world?

Some U.S. foreign direct investment is destined for low-income countries, to help manufacture inputs that will be ultimately used for assembly in America or other countries. But as figure 2-12 shows, the overwhelming bulk of direct investment abroad by Americans has gone to rich countries. Indeed, one recent study documents that as of

Figure 2-12. Destinations of U.S. Foreign Direct Investment, 1996

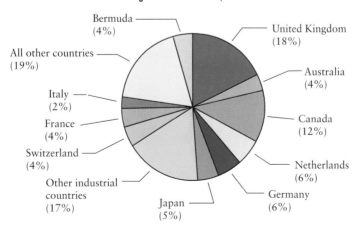

Bermuda
(4%)

All other countries
(19%)

Italy
(2%)

France
(4%)

Switzerland
(4%)

Other industrial
countries
(17%)

Japan
(5%)

United Kingdom
(18%)

Australia
(4%)

Canada
(12%)

Netherlands
(6%)

Germany
(6%)

Source: Quinlan (1997b).

Figure 2-13. Compositions of U.S. Foreign Direct Investment., 1996

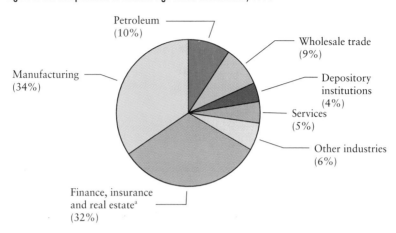

Source: Data are from the Bureau of Economic Analysis, accessed on the bureau's worldwide web page.
a. Finance does not include banking

1992, only one-third of U.S.-owned multinational companies had any production activities in developing countries.[14] Furthermore, as shown in figure 2-13, Americans invest abroad in very much the same sectors as do foreigners in the United States, with both manufacturing and finance ranking at the top of the list.

It would be difficult, if not impossible, to devise practical methods for restricting either direct or portfolio investments overseas. One might be able to prevent or restrain General Motors from building automobile plants in developing countries or purchasing automobile parts from abroad. But American laws and tradition would make it very hard to stop banks, insurance companies, mutual funds, and private individuals from investing abroad in the same kinds of plants. Moreover, once such plants had been established, little could be done to stop the companies that owned them from hiring American experts to help design and run the plants or market their products.

14. Brainard and Riker (1997). Furthermore, the same authors find that the output levels of affiliates in developing countries and in industrialized countries tend to move together, which suggests that multinational companies are dividing their production activities by skill requirements; see Riker and Brainard (1997).

Benefits of Immigration

Not only goods and capital move across national borders. People do so as well. America has long been a magnet for people from all over world. It is a country offering political freedom and seemingly unbounded economic opportunity. Successive waves of immigrants have come to improve their lives, and at the same time, to enrich the economic and political fabric of the United States.

From a strictly economic point of view, the case for a liberal immigration policy rests on several arguments. Immigrants have historically been hard working, entrepreneurial, and high saving—all traits valued strongly by Americans. Immigration augments the working-age population, and thus helps to counter the looming financial problem of funding government programs for the retired elderly, notably, social security and medicare.

In recent years, however, immigration—especially illegal immigration—has become a divisive political issue. Opponents claim that immigrants have a higher propensity to commit crimes and draw welfare payments. Many come with limited educational qualifications, and these immigrants compete in the labor market with native-born Americans who have few skills, arguably reducing their employment rates and depressing their wages. In a comprehensive analysis of immigration in the United States, the National Academy of Sciences recently examined these claims and concluded that, in general, any negative impacts of recent immigration trends have not been signficant; indeed, immigration has provided modest economic benefits to the nation as a whole.[15]

Nonetheless, as with trade, not every U.S. citizen is a "winner" from immigration. The losers are found especially among those who compete most directly with recent immigrants, particularly less-skilled native workers. In chapter 4 we discuss this impact of immigration in greater detail.

No country has a totally open policy toward immigration in the same way that some countries do have open policies toward trade and investment. There are social and political limits to how quickly and to

---

15. Smith and Edmonston (1997).

what extent countries can absorb people with different cultural and linguistic backgrounds. Nonetheless, it is important to keep in mind that just as foreign investors who bring money to the United States often also bring know-how with them, many immigrants bring talents and values that are American at their very core. The challenge for the United States in the future is to decide who those immigrants will be.

The Globaphobic Critique

Despite the advantages of openness and increased economic linkages with other countries, attacks have been mounted from several different directions against globalization and the policies that have encouraged it. In the 1980s the critique was fairly narrow and, by today's standards, rather mild. The United States was said to be competing on an "unlevel playing field" with other countries that maintained far higher barriers to trade and investment. Fair trade, not free trade was the slogan of the day. In the 1990s, the entire trend toward globalization has come under attack, charged with robbing Americans of their jobs and suppressing their wages, especially the wages of those with the fewest skills. Many critics do not stop there. As a result of the 1994 Uruguay Round trade agreement that created the World Trade Organization, they allege, the United States has sacrificed part of its sovereignty. Meanwhile, others point to a new kind of unlevel playing field, marked by lax standards governing labor and the environment rather than by barriers to trade and investment. How, they ask, can the United States be expected to conclude trade deals with countries that do not recognize unions, that employ children in unsafe jobs, and that despoil the environment with reckless abandon?

While the details of some of the present criticisms of openness may be new, the broad contours of the attack are not. In fact, the merits and drawbacks of open economic policy have been debated since the earliest days of the Republic. Benjamin Franklin, for example, once wrote that commerce should be "as free between all the nations of the world, as it is between the several counties of England," and John Adams declared, "I am against all shackles upon trade." Alexander Hamilton, whose views we have discussed, was perhaps the most forceful early advocate of the opposite view. The debate has continued for over two hundred years. Yet, with some well-known interruptions, the proponents of openness have generally been on the winning side (although sometimes for the wrong reasons). Whether they continue to win the policy debate will be determined by the strengths and weaknesses of the modern case for maintaining and extending an open economic policy. In the following chapters, we address the attacks made by today's critics of globalization.

3 OPENNESS AND JOBS

Much of the debate about trade is about jobs. Critics say that it destroys them, while proponents say it creates them. Both are wrong. This chapter explains why.

Job Destruction versus Job Creation

The claim that freer trade destroys jobs may seem persuasive at first glance. If Americans buy a foreign-made car or television, that is one less car or television made by a plant in the United States (whether owned by Americans or foreigners). Multiply the example many times, and many fewer Americans will have jobs making cars, televisions, and virtually everything else that Americans import.

To trade critics, the low wages that workers earn in some other countries strengthen this logic. How can a U.S. company in any industry compete against firms that pay their workers only a few dollars an hour—or even, a few dollars a day! No wonder Ross Perot warned of the "great sucking sound" of U.S. jobs going to Mexico when the United States entered into the North American Free Trade Agreement (NAFTA). Once all remaining trade barriers were removed, Perot argued, millions of jobs would "run" to Mexico.

To make matters worse, the critics argue, more U.S. jobs are lost when American companies, realizing all the money they can save in labor costs, move their plants to countries with very low wages. Multinational companies, even those owned or based in America, are thus apparently just as guilty of job destruction as the foreign companies that ship their products here.

Some proponents of freer trade, although they may not explicitly recognize it, agree with the critics on the premise that the right way to argue about trade is in terms of whether it destroys or creates jobs. How many times, for example, has one heard a high-level administration official or member of Congress assert that a particular trade agreement will generate so many billion dollars of additional exports, which translates into so many more thousands of jobs? They are advised to argue this way by pollsters and other political pundits, who say that Americans can only understand that free trade is beneficial if it is sold as a way to generate new jobs.

It turns out, however, that both sides of this debate ignore some basic economic principles and facts. Trade is not about generating more or fewer jobs, but generating better jobs and a higher national standard of living.

The Truth about Trade and Jobs

It is tempting for critics of trade to liken the economy to a balloon. When consumers in this country buy foreign imports and send out money or obligations to pay for them, are they not simply letting air out of the balloon? Is it not the case that national income and total employment must shrink?

Actually, the answer is no, because there are other sources of economic demand that replace any that may be lost through imports. For one, when the outflow of dollars from the United States to pay for imports is larger in volume than the inflow of dollars from the sale of U.S. exports, the larger supply of dollars on world exchange markets pushes the value of the dollar down (just as a larger supply of apples or oranges would push down their prices). A lower dollar makes U.S. exports more competitive on world markets. After a lag of several months, the increased demand for exports pumps air into the economy's balloon to replace that lost through imports, in the process shifting production and employment away from the goods and services that the United States is comparatively poor at producing and toward higher value exports.[1] Indeed, jobs in exporting firms and industries pay wages that are about 5 to 15 percent above the national average for precisely this reason: they are more productive than average (and certainly more productive than the jobs in industries that are shrinking as a result of imports from developing countries).[2]

The Federal Reserve is another source of replacement air for the balloon. The Fed projects (although not perfectly) exports, imports, and other components of national output in setting monetary policy. If the governors of the Federal Reserve believe total output, including net exports, will grow too slowly to accommodate the increase in the labor force, they will pump additional money into the economy, assuming that inflation is not increasing or already too high. Adding to the supply of money reduces interest rates, stimulating higher spending by consumers and businesses, which can offset any contractionary impact of higher imports. Conversely, if the Fed believes that total output will grow too rapidly to be consistent with stable inflation, it will slow the pace of money creation in order to reign in spending—regardless of the level of imports.

The effects just described work in reverse when there is an increase in exports. Stronger export performance, other things being equal, leads to an appreciation of the currency, which makes foreign goods cheaper for domestic residents and thus encourages imports. Moreover, if stronger exports lead the Fed to believe that overall aggregate demand, including exports, is increasing too rapidly to be consistent with stable inflation, it will raise interest rates to take some of the steam out of the

---

1. If exchange rates are fixed, the offsetting effects of higher exports work through the domestic price level, albeit more slowly. Assuming that the Federal Reserve does not pursue a countervailing expansionary policy, a rise in imports that comes at the expense of domestic production reduces the demand for labor, while putting downward pressure on prices of competing domestically produced goods. In combination, the two effects damp inflation, over time enhancing the competitiveness of U.S. exports in world markets and making it easier for the Federal Reserve to be expansive, as described in the text.

2. See Richardson and Rindal (1996).

economy. The net effect is that the additional exports will not lead to any more than a temporary increase in overall employment.[3]

In reality, of course, it is misleading to think of the economic balloon as static in size, with air simply going in and going out in balanced amounts. The productive capacity of the economy—and thus the potential size of the economic balloon—is constantly growing, at a rate determined by the sum of the growth rates of the labor force and of labor productivity. Most economists believe the potential growth rate of the economy is now somewhere between 2 and 2.5 percent. The main job of the Federal Reserve is to keep the economy growing at that proper pace—or at a faster rate, if it is recovering from a recession. The key point, however, is that economic growth and employment can keep growing regardless of the level or trend in imports. Over the medium to long run the balloon does not shrink because imports grow.

Admittedly, our balloon analogy must be qualified in at least two respects. Trade flows can have effects on aggregate output in the *short run* if the economy is operating at less than full capacity and if the Federal Reserve does not take action to deliberately offset those effects. At this writing, however, the U.S. economy is effectively at full employment and so even the "Asian flu" that is expected to reduce U.S. exports and enlarge imports from that region cannot be blamed for reducing U.S. output and employment. The reason is that had the Asian crisis not occurred, the Fed was poised to raise interest rates to restrain domestic demand. The Fed would have acted to prevent growing tightness in labor markets from leading to accelerating wage and price inflation. The problems in Asia essentially let the Fed off the hook.

In addition, imports can and do affect jobs in *particular* industries or firms. Trade, like changes in technology, moves jobs around: toward products in which a nation has a comparative advantage and away from products where the comparative advantage lies overseas. Defenders of freer trade have traditionally argued that those who lose from trade by losing jobs can and should be compensated for their difficulties by the winners: consumers, and perhaps workers who find bet-

---

3. As discussed in chapter 5, the same logic explains why the removal of foreign barriers to U.S. exports also does not increase total employment in the medium to long run.

ter jobs in export industries. In our concluding chapter we suggest that too often economists and policymakers alike pay only lip service to this proposition. Accordingly, we outline a plan that would take the compensation principle much more seriously.

The Evidence

All of this may sound like abstract theorizing, but it is not. Not much sophistication is needed to rebut the claim that trade lowers total employment. Even as the United States has become more global during this decade, the economy has grown steadily, and in the process has generated more than 14 million additional jobs. The result, as noted in the introductory chapter, is the lowest national unemployment rate in over twenty-five years.

Is the same true over a longer period? Figure 3-1 unequivocally answers yes. The figure shows that as a percentage of national output, the sum of imports and exports rose from 9 percent in 1960 to over 24 percent by the mid-1990s. Yet the fraction of Americans of working age who have a job has continued grow, rising to new highs in every recent business expansion. Whereas only 55 percent of adults were employed in 1950, nearly 64 percent held jobs in 1997.

We do not make the bold claim that employment has risen because of closer integration of the U.S. economy with the rest of the world. Most of the increase has come about because American women increasingly have wanted to work. Yet it is noteworthy that the big jump in women's employment occurred at the same time as U.S. trade expanded—increased trade did not prevent women from getting jobs.

Some American workers do lose their jobs as a result of the inroads of foreign producers. But at the same time, as just described, jobs are created in other sectors of the economy, whether in industries making goods and services for export or in firms producing output for domestic consumption. As a result, there is no long-term relation between the national unemployment rate—which is determined by the health of the overall economy rather than of the firms in competition with foreign producers—and the volume of imports. This fact is demonstrated by figure 3-2. While imports' share of the national income more than

Figure 3-1. Growth of U.S. Trade and Employment, 1960–97

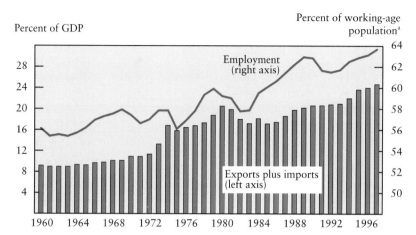

Source: Data from Bureau of Economic Analysis and Bureau of Labor Statistics.
a. Ages sixteen years and older.

tripled between 1960 and 1996, the unemployment rate fluctuated but showed very little overall trend. The jobless rate was roughly 5.5 percent in both 1960 and 1996.

Equally significant, neither trade nor its absence can shelter a country from wide cycles in unemployment. The longest and most severe contraction of the twentieth century was the Great Depression, when imports and exports represented a very small percentage of the U.S. economy. Economic historians believe that the severity, duration, and worldwide scope of the Great Depression was partly the result of a sharp curtailment of global trade that resulted from greater protection, of which the Hawley-Smoot Tariff Act of 1930 was a prime and leading example.

In recent years the relationship between imports, exports, and U.S. employment has been almost precisely the opposite of that predicted by critics of free trade, as is shown in figure 3-3. The lower line in the figure shows that since the late 1970s, net exports—the difference between the value of goods and services that U.S. producers sell in overseas markets and the value of goods and services that foreign producers sell in the United States—as a share of total output has been consistently negative, although since its sharp fall in the first half of the

Figure 3-2. U.S. Imports and Unemployment, 1960–97

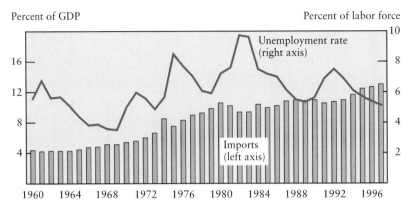

Source: Data from Department of Commerce (National Income and Product Accounts concept) and Bureau of Labor Statistics.

1980s there has been noticeable improvement. Yet the upper line of the figure illustrates that in all but two years of this period, total employment increased. Indeed, the change in total employment appears as the mirror image of the current account deficit.

The negative relationship between employment and the nation's trade performance may seem surprising to noneconomists. But if one

Figure 3-3. U.S. Net Exports and Growth in Employment, 1979–96

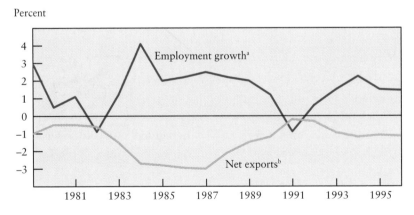

Source: Data from Bureau of Economic Analysis and Bureau of Labor Statistics.
a. Percent per year.
b. Percent of GDP.

stops and thinks about it for a moment, the relationship is easy to understand. Both the trade deficit and employment growth are linked to the American business cycle. When overall U.S. demand rises strongly, consumers and businesses seek to increase their purchases from all available suppliers, both domestic and foreign. This tends to boost American companies' demand for workers, increasing the employment rate, and to push U.S. imports up faster than exports. The process is reversed when U.S. demand for goods and services contracts, as it does in a recession.

The demand for U.S. exports in other countries is subject to a similar cycle. Strong overall demand in a particular country tends to lift U.S. exports faster than imports. But the United States has dozens of important trade partners, each with a distinctive business cycle pattern. Consequently, the U.S. cycle of rising and falling trade deficits tends to mirror the overall level of demand in the United States rather than that in any particular foreign economy. Figure 3-3 shows this typically means that the deficit increases when U.S. employment soars, and shrinks when demand for new workers is weak or contracting.

Openness and Manufacturing Jobs

Even if trade does not reduce overall employment, many Americans worry that it destroys good jobs in the manufacturing industries that compete most directly with imports. A good job is easy to describe. It offers excellent wages and fringe benefits, healthy prospects of promotion, pleasant working conditions, and long-term job security. According to popular wisdom, manufacturing once offered such jobs to millions of workers, most of whom had no educational credentials beyond a high school diploma. Critics of free trade argue that imports have made such jobs unnecessary in the United States, thus blocking the traditional path to the middle class for Americans from modest backgrounds.

Statistics on job growth clearly support the claim that manufacturing's importance in employment has slipped. As shown by figure 3-4, in the 1950s manufacturing accounted for about one-third of all payroll jobs. It now provides only about one job in seven to workers on

Figure 3-4. Manufacturing as a Share of the U.S. Economy, 1959–94

Percent

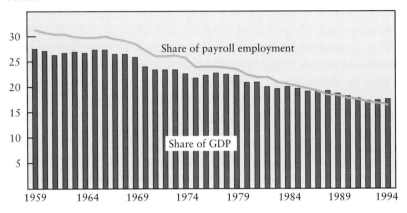

Source: Council of Economic Advisers (1997).

nonfarm payrolls. It is easy to exaggerate the importance of a shrinking manufacturing base in the loss of good jobs, however. The total number of payroll jobs in manufacturing has fluctuated between 18 million and 21 million since the mid-1960s, with the current level near the low end of that range. But manufacturing offers reasonably good jobs, especially to workers with average or below-average schooling. Hourly wages in manufacturing are about 9 percent higher than wages in other private sector jobs. If the manufacturing sector were larger, average wages would be somewhat higher, especially for workers with limited schooling.

The absolute level of manufacturing employment has declined much more slowly than the sector's share in total employment. A major reason for this relative fall in manufacturing employment is that manufactured goods account for a dwindling percentage of Americans' consumption. As people's incomes rise, they tend to spend an increasing percentage of their incomes on health, education, and other kinds of services and a smaller percentage on manufactured goods. Figure 3-4 also shows that the decline in the manufacturing employment share parallels the decline in manufacturing's share of total output. Short of forcing Americans to buy steel I-beams and household appliances and rationing their consumption of hospital services and restaurant meals, it is hard to see how this long-term trend can be reversed. Indeed, the same trends are visible in other countries, even those with a much lower living standard than the United States. Figure 3-5 illustrates that services—nonmanufactured output—have increased their share of overall output in both industrialized and developing or emerging market countries between 1980 and 1994. Clearly, the relative decline of manufacturing and the corresponding rise of services would occur with or without world economic integration.

The manufacturing share in employment also has declined because of the continued success of manufacturing industries in boosting worker productivity. Figure 3-6 shows that in the early postwar period measured productivity in the entire business sector grew at approximately the same pace as productivity in manufacturing. However, since 1973 productivity growth has edged down in manufacturing, but it has plunged in other sectors of the economy, especially in the service sector.

A simple comparison demonstrates the powerful impact on jobs of differential productivity in different parts of the economy. According to government statistics, steelworkers were 125 percent more productive in 1995 than in 1973. In contrast, the productivity of workers in the hotel and motel industry improved by just 11 percent over this period.[4] These numbers mean that employment could only have grown at equal rates in the steel and lodging industries if the demand for steel had climbed at least ten times faster than the demand for hotel accommodations. However, the demand for lodging in fact nearly doubled between 1973 and 1995, while demand for steel remained roughly unchanged. Fast productivity growth combined with slow growth in demand meant that many jobs in the steel industry disappeared. In contrast, slow productivity growth combined with rapid growth in the demand for accommodations meant that hotels and motels added hundreds of thousands of workers to their payrolls.

These powerful domestic trends necessarily imply that any role played by international trade in the decline of manufacturing employment must have been small. Figure 3-7 confirms this to be the case. The blue line illustrates the steep drop in the percentage of payroll workers employed in manufacturing. The orange line in the chart shows, however, that only a very small portion of the decline in manufacturing employment would have been avoided if the entire trade deficit after

4. "Industry Productivity," http://stats.bls.gov/iprhome.htm

Figure 3-5. Services as a Share of GDP, Selected Countries, 1980 and 1994

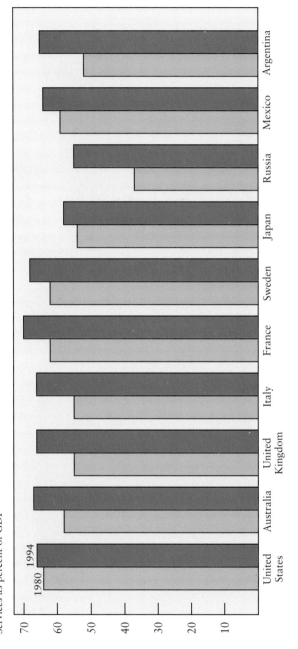

Services as percent of GDP

Figure 3-6. Productivity Growth in U.S. Manufacturing and Business Sector, 1959–95

Annual percentage change

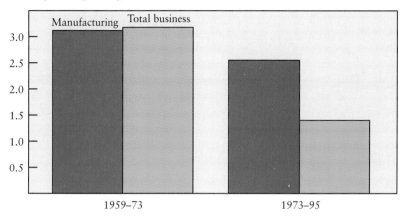

Source: Council of Economic Advisers (1997).

1975 had been eliminated through extra production of U.S. manufactured goods. Under this very generous assumption, the payrolls of manufacturing companies would have been about 8 percent larger in 1994 than they in fact were; so that instead of falling 15 percentage points over the period 1960–94, manufacturing employment would have fallen 14 percentage points (to 17 percent of nonfarm payrolls).

Figure 3-7. Manufacturing as a Share of Total U.S. Employment, 1960–94

Percent of payroll employment

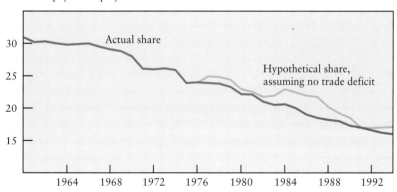

Source: Authors' calculations based on Council of Economic Advisers (1997).

The small change in the composition of employment, in turn, would have had a very small effect on average wages, a subject to which we turn in the next chapter. Assuming the pay differential between manufacturing and nonmanufacturing workers were maintained, the average private sector wage would have risen just 2 cents an hour, or about one-tenth of a percent. Even if good jobs were disappearing in the American economy, which they are not, eliminating the trade deficit by restricting imports would not bring them back.

NAFTA, Jobs, and the Great Sucking Sound

In recent years, the debate about trade and jobs was perhaps most heated when the United States and Canada invited Mexico to join the North American Free Trade Agreement. Like so many public policy debates, the argument in 1993 over Mexico's entry into NAFTA was characterized by hyperbole on both sides.

Some advocates argued that extending NAFTA would be a job-generation bonanza for American workers. Critics argued the opposite, claiming that low wages would allow Mexico to become an export machine, destroying hundreds of thousands of American jobs. This was the specter of the "great sucking sound" popularized by Ross Perot.

The claims about NAFTA's effect on jobs were misleading. A country of Mexico's size—its total GDP in 1993 was less than 5 percent of U.S. GDP, while its nonoil exports represented well under 1 percent of U.S. GDP—could not have been expected to have had a significant overall impact on the U.S. economy. Furthermore, tariffs on either side of the border were not particularly high when the agreement was signed: 10 percent in Mexico and 4 percent in the United States. Elimination of these tariffs could not have been expected to cause large shifts in trade. And the claim that American firms would relocate en masse to Mexico must bow to the fact that even after NAFTA went into effect, U.S. direct investment in Mexico totals about $3 billion a year, up by only about $1 billion since before the agreement, and small compared to the more than $700 billion that American firms currently spend on plant and equipment in the United States.

Since Mexico joined NAFTA, critics and supporters of the treaty have traded estimates of its impact on jobs. By any reasonable measure, even the gross job turnover induced by the agreement has been slight. According to the Department of Labor, over the nearly four years from January 1994 through mid-August 1997, 220,000 workers had petitioned it for adjustment assistance (cash and training allowances) under legislation enacted when the trade deal was signed. Of this total, 136,000—an average of about 40,000 workers per year—were certified as eligible for assistance (under both the more general trade adjustment assistance program and that created as part of NAFTA). Even this figure overstates NAFTA's true impact, because to be eligible under both programs workers only need to show that "imports" have contributed to their losses, but not specifically as a result of NAFTA. By way of comparison, the gross monthly turnover of jobs in the United States exceeds 2 million. Since NAFTA, overall employment in the United States has risen by more than 10 million.

The debate about jobs and NAFTA is a side-show, because the dominant reason why Mexico wanted to join NAFTA and why the United States (and Canada) agreed to its entry had little to do with economics in the United States. To be sure, some large American firms saw potential for increased business opportunities in Mexico. But the idea originated with Mexico's Carlos Salinas, who, as a one-term president under Mexican law, wanted to lock in his promarket reforms so that they could not be reversed by his successors. The United States not only shared this objective, but also could hardly say no to a country that until then had deep suspicions of its northern neighbor, was the source of heavy illegal immigration, and was a trans-shipment point for drugs flowing into America. In short, the United States has long had, and continues to have, a strategic interest in a prosperous Mexico.

As it turned out, Salinas succeeded in locking in liberalization, although hardly in the manner that he intended. When Mexico fell into a deep recession in the aftermath of peso crisis of late 1994, it did not raise barriers to U.S. goods, as it had during its economic troubles of the early 1980s. In consequence, as shown in figure 3-8, U.S. exports actually increased slightly in 1995, while those from other countries took a nose dive, allowing the United States to gain a larger

Figure 3-8. Percentage Change in Exports to Mexico, 1994–95

Percentage change

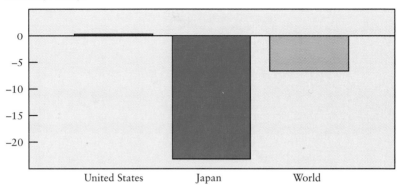

Source: *International Trade Statistics Yearbook*, 1995.

share of Mexico's overall imports: 71 percent compared with 68 percent in 1994. By 1996, the U.S. export share had increased to 72 percent; while in absolute terms, the U.S. total of $67 billion outpaced its
1994 level of $57 billion.[5]

The North American Free Trade Agreement has one other important
lesson—for political leaders who have been accustomed to selling trade
agreements on the basis of their alleged impact on job creation. In the
case of NAFTA, this traditional strategy backfired, especially after the
Mexican economy tumbled and the United States had to mount (an
ultimately successful and profitable) financial rescue. Indeed, discom-
fort over NAFTA has since played a significant role in souring the public mood toward freer trade in general. The moral of this story is that it
does not pay to use bad economic arguments, even to sell good policies.

5. Bhagwati (1997).

4 OPENNESS AND WAGES

The argument that growing trade must hurt employment and boost overall joblessness in the United States does not survive even casual examination of the evidence. American employment has surged. The jobless rate has fallen steadily in the 1990s—at this writing, hovering near 4.5 percent, the lowest in a generation—in spite of a massive increase in imports and exports. Aware of these developments, critics of globalization in recent years have focused on a different line of attack: that the combination of increased trade, more outward investment, and additional immigration have depressed the wages of American workers while aggravating income inequalities.

That wage growth has slowed and wages have become more unequal cannot be denied. The bottom line in figure 4-1 illustrates that after rising at a healthy pace until the early 1970s, average hourly earnings (excluding fringe benefits) among nonagricultural workers have actually fallen, adjusting for consumer price inflation. To make matters worse, wages have been getting more unequal throughout this period. Figure 4-2 shows, for example, that in 1973 men at the ninetieth percentile of the wage distribution earned roughly 3.5 times the wage of men in the tenth percentile. For women, this ratio was slightly lower. By 1996, however, the wage ratio of workers at the ninetieth

Figure 4-1. Growth of U.S. Wages and Productivity, 1959–96

Index, 1959 = 1

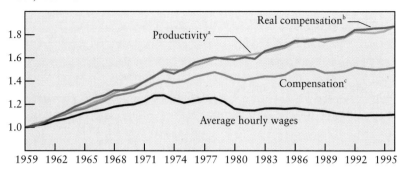

Source: U.S. Department of Labor (1997); and Council of Economic Advisers (1997).
a. Nonfarm business.
b. Using nonfarm business implicit price deflator.
c. Using CPI deflator.

percentile relative to the workers at the tenth percentile had climbed to 4.5 for men and 4.0 for women.

The question that this chapter examines is whether and to what extent openness, in all its dimensions, is responsible for these disturbing developments.

Figure 4-2. Ratio of Hourly Pay at Top to Pay at Bottom of U.S. Wage Distribution, 1973–96

Ratio[a]

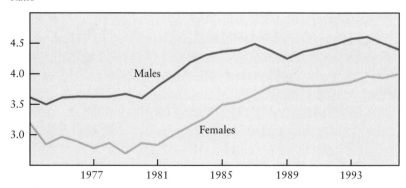

Source: Census Bureau's Current Population Survey outgoing rotation samples, as estimated by Employment Policy Institute.
a. Ratio of ninetieth percentile to tenth percentile wage.

The Critics' Case

The logic behind the claim that increased trade is largely responsible for slower wage growth and rising wage inequality would seem to be impeccable. If Americans can freely buy goods made by workers in other countries, then are not U.S. workers effectively in the same labor pool as workers overseas? If so, then does not trade expand the supply of workers without changing the demand for their products, thereby forcing down the wages of U.S. workers? And is this downward pressure not especially severe for the lowest paid U.S. workers, whose limited skills place them in head-to-head competition with unskilled workers abroad?

The critics of openness can seemingly draw on sophisticated economic theory to support their claims. In the first half of this century two Swedish economists, Eli Hecksher and Bertil Ohlin, developed a theory to explain the pattrn of international trade among countries in which there were important differences in the relative abundance of different factors of production, such as labor, capital equpment, and natural resources. MIT economist Paul Samuelson extended this theory in the 1940s to show that free trade between two countries that share the same production technology will not only drive the prices of goods they trade to identical levels, but will do the same for the prices of key factors of production: the wage earned by workers and the rate of return earned by owners of capital.[1] The logic behind this "factor equalization theorem" is plain enough: if workers with similar skills around the world compete in a common market, their wages should be the same.[2] Critics of liberal trade use this result to suggest that when the United States trades freely with Mexico or the Philippines, where wages are far lower, U.S. wages must be driven down to the levels prevailing in those poor countries.

Another strand of economic theory appears to support the claim that removal of trade barriers has been particularly disadvantageous for the least-skilled workers, who earn low wages in the United States but even lower wages in developing countries. Building on the insights

1. Samuelson (1948, pp. 163–84).
2. At the same time, the return on capital, adjusted to reflect different levels of risk, will be equalized.

of Hecksher and Ohlin, American economists Wolfgang Stolper and Paul Samuelson demonstrated in the 1940s that the increase of a domestic price of a product, brought about by a higher tariff on the product, will increase the price of the factor of production that is heavily used in producing that product.[3] The Stolper-Samuelson result implies, for example, that if shoes are produced mainly with the labor of unskilled workers, an increase in the tariff on imported shoes will tend to increase the wages earned by unskilled workers. Of course, the theory also implies the opposite result: *removal* of the tariff on imported shoes will *reduce* the wages of unskilled workers. If all workers have roughly the same level of skill, then removal of the tariff will reduce the average wage earned by *all* workers.

To critics of openness, overseas investment by U.S. firms adds to the injury suffered by American workers. By fleeing to other low-wage locations, or even threatening to do so, firms can seemingly pressure their workers to accept lower wages—at the very least, to refrain from demanding pay increases. Capital is "footloose," while labor is immobile. Labor cannot stand a chance in this environment, they say, and must inevitably lose bargaining power. The wage suppression arguments of the 1990s have strong parallels to critics' claims in the 1980s that trade was turning good jobs into lousy ones. That was when Democratic presidential candidate Walter Mondale and others decried the fact that the United States was losing manufacturing jobs to foreigners (notably Japan) and was at risk of becoming a nation of hamburger flippers and dry cleaners.

The trade critics of the 1990s, however, see even greater dangers ahead. They observe that virtually all future population growth will take place in countries like China, India, and Indonesia, where wages are a fraction of those in the United States. At the same time, highly mobile capital is increasingly finding its way to these places, arming third-world workers with first world technology. The end result seems inevitable: the United States and other industrialized countries will be overwhelmed with cheap, but high-quality, manufactured items that will ultimately destroy their own manufacturing industries. Even if that does not occur, workers in all sectors of the U.S. economy face the

3. Stolper and Samuelson (1941).

prospect of their wages eroding, because workers in both the service and manufacturing sectors are part of a single national labor pool.

Openness and Average Wages

If globalization, or forces external to the U.S. economy, were somehow responsible for the disappointing growth in average wages, one would expect to see a growing gap between the productivity of American workers and what these workers are paid. That is, if is true that factor price equalization is driving wages in first world economies down toward those earned in the third world, and that threats by U.S. companies to move to other locations are reinforcing this effect, then average wage growth should be lagging behind worker productivity. This has not occurred. Productivity and labor compensation (properly measured) have changed at about the same pace. Average compensation is rising at a slower pace than before 1973 for a simple reason: productivity also is not growing as rapidly as it once did.

Nonetheless, at least at first glance, figure 4-1 seems to be inconsistent with these propositions: there has been a growing disparity between *hourly wages* (the bottom line) and productivity (the top line). But appearances can often be deceiving, and a closer look at the same figure reveals why. The simple comparison between hourly wages and productivity ignores the fact that most workers receive not only cash wages, but also a package of fringe benefits, including health insurance and retirement benefits. Figure 4-1 shows a much closer connection between the growth in *total compensation* (the second line from the bottom) and productivity.

It is also critical to adjust the actual dollar value of compensation per hour at any given time by an appropriate measure of inflation. The hourly wages illustrated by the bottom line of figure 4-1 are deflated only by the change in prices of the goods and services that Americans consume. But overall national productivity includes goods and services sold both for consumption and for investment. In recent years, productivity has grown at a slower pace in consumer goods industries than in the industries making machinery and equipment (particularly computers). When total compensation is measured in terms of workers' purchasing power over *all* the goods and services they produce—both those that are purchased for consumption and those purchased for investment—figure 4-1 shows (second line from the top) that real compensation growth has essentially matched growth in productivity.

Executives may blame foreign competition or threaten to move abroad during labor negotiations, but to understand what drives the economy, one needs to listen to facts, not anecdotes. And the facts reveal that whereas both productivity and hourly compensation grew faster than 2.5 percent annually from 1959 to 1973, annual real compensation growth (based on prices of output in the nonfarm business sector) has slumped to about 1 percent since 1973. There is no mystery about why wages and compensation have grown more slowly over the past two decades: compensation growth fell because productivity growth declined at virtually the same rate. The trends in trade played only a small role, at best, in the trend toward lower productivity growth.[4]

We underscore the adjective "measured" to describe productivity trends, because in recent years questions have been raised about the accuracy of the index the government uses to measure price changes in the economy. The 1996 Boskin Report on the Bureau of Labor Statistics' Consumer Price Index, for example, concluded that current procedures overstate the rate of price inflation by about 1.1 percent per year. If there is an overstatement of the inflation rate, it must mean that the rates of growth of real output, productivity, and compensation have been understated by an equivalent amount (since price indexes are used to deflate the nominal measures of output in order to compute an inflation-adjusted, or "real," level of output).

In fact, there has been much controversy over the conclusions of the Boskin Report. Many economists believe that while current price indexes may modestly overstate inflation, the errors are not nearly as large as the report suggests. Furthermore, although one of the report's central criticisms was the need to make significant adjustments for improvements in the quality of goods, government statisticians already do this, and they are continually working to further refine their meth-

4. If anything, for the reasons discussed in the previous chapter, the increasing globalization of the U.S. economy should have enhanced productivity growth, and thus the rate of growth of real compensation.

Figure 4-3. U.S. National Income by Type of Income, 1959–96

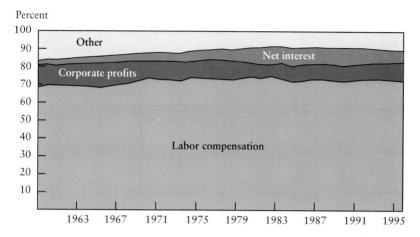

Source: National Income and Product Accounts, various years.

ods.[5] But whatever the precise degree of understatement of the measures of productivity and real compensation, the errors relating to quality affect those measures *in all years*, not only in the recent decades when the rates of growth in productivity and compensation have slowed. In short, those who believe that U.S. compensation growth has slowed are certainly correct, regardless of the mismeasurement of the CPI.

Some critics of globalization nevertheless point to the growing profitability of American business in the 1990s as evidence that U.S. workers have been short-changed as a result of foreign competition. On the surface, this claim, too, has an element of plausibility. If shareholders are receiving a larger portion of the economic pie, then by definition, workers are surely receiving a smaller slice. Globalization would seem to be the natural explanation for the changing division between capitalists and workers.

Again, however, it is important to look at the facts. Figure 4-3 shows what has happened since 1959 to labor compensation and other types

5. Barry Bosworth and Jack Triplett at the Brookings Institution are currently heading a multiyear project on ways to improve the measurement of output and inflation in the service sector, where many (if not most) of the alleged measurement problems lie. They are working with government statisticians and economists as well as researchers from universities and the private sector.

of income, measured as shares of national income. The figure illustrates that the profit share has indeed risen in the 1990s, but remains smaller than it was the 1960s. Moreover, the other component of income going to owners of capital, interest payments, has fallen in the 1990s due to lower interest rates. As for labor compensation, its share has not fallen: in 1996 it actually was a bit higher than in the late 1950s and early 1960s. (Of course, while labor as a whole may have slightly more of the economic pie, certain groups of workers and individual workers certainly have lost ground). In sum, there is no substance to the claim that, on average, workers are getting a smaller share of the American economic pie. The problem is that the pie itself is not growing as rapidly as it once did. But for this development, trade bears no responsibility.

Average Wages and Trade with Low-Wage Countries

What about the claim that imports from low-wage countries are hurting American workers? Putting aside for the moment the notion that competition from developing countries must be especially harmful to lesser skilled U.S. workers, surely the fact that many countries pay their workers only a fraction of U.S. wages must be dampening the average compensation earned by Americans. The evidence about trends in compensation, productivity, and shares of national income may be too remote to resonate with most people. Is there other evidence that bears more directly on the influence of trade on wages? Fortunately, there is a variety of other data.

First, simple comparisons of U.S. wages with those paid by other countries are highly misleading if they do not also reflect the differences in productivity of workers in different countries. Figure 4-4 illustrates a very close relationship between the cost of labor in manufacturing and average worker productivity (measured as gross domestic product per capita) in various countries in 1985. *The figure demonstrates that wages in poor countries are low because worker productivity in these countries is low.* This low productivity is not surprising, since workers in poor countries are not as educated as U.S. workers, do not have the advantages of working with sophisticated factory

Figure 4-4. Labor Productivity and Labor Costs, Selected Countries, 1985

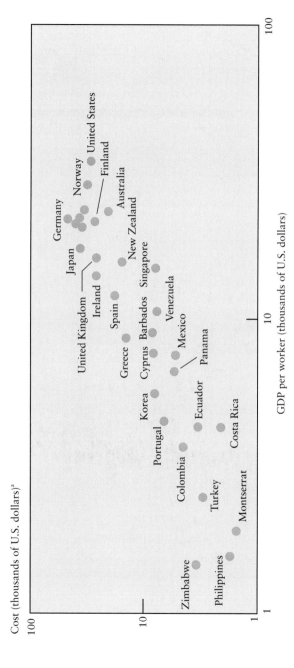

Cost (thousands of U.S. dollars)[a]

GDP per worker (thousands of U.S. dollars)

Source: Rodrik (1997b).
a. Manufacturing labor.

Figure 4-5. U. S. Imports by Source, 1978–96

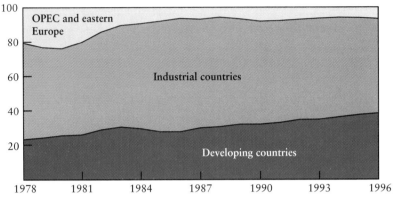

Percent of total imports

Source: Council of Economic Advisers (1997, table B-103).

equipment or in an economy with a modern infrastructure (good roads and up-to-date computers and telecommunications), and, in many cases, live under governments that put roadblocks in the way of economic innovation and improvement.

Second, while the United States certainly trades with developing countries that pay much lower wages than those received by U.S. workers, most of its imports are produced in developed countries, as shown in figure 4-5. Developing country imports are becoming more important, and now constitute nearly 40 percent of the total. But since total imports represent just 12 percent of national output, developing country imports account for less than 5 percent of national output. Thus even if imports from low-wage countries were driving down the average U.S. wage—which we dispute—the small share of these imports relative to the size of the overall economy implies that any such impact must be small.

Third, even as imports from developing countries have increased, so have wages in these countries, relative to those in the United States. As shown in figure 4-6, in 1960 the average nonindustrialized country paid only a little more than 10 percent of the manufacturing wages received by workers in the United States. By 1992, wages in developing countries had risen to about 30 percent of U.S. manufacturing wages, reflecting improvements in productivity in those countries. At

Figure 4-6. Wages of U.S. Trading Partners as a Share of U.S. Wages, Manufacturing

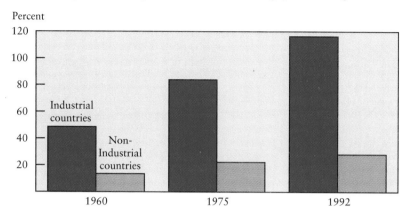

Percent

1960   1975   1992

Sources: Susan Collins's calculations, based on International Labor Organization, *Yearbook of Labor Statistics*, various years; and International Monetary Fund, *Direction of Trade Statistics Yearbook*, various years.

the same time, manufacturing wages in industrialized countries also were increasing faster than in the United States, so that by 1992 they had exceeded U.S. wages. Indeed, figure 4-7 shows that in 1996 hourly compensation in U.S. manufacturing was well below that in some of its major trading partners. If American firms cannot compete successfully with German firms in selling chemicals to Latin America or with Japanese companies in selling automobiles to Southeast Asia, their failures certainly cannot be traced to low wages in Germany or Japan. The simultaneous increase in wages in both the developed and the less developed worlds is reflected in figure 4-8, which shows that the weighted average compensation in manufacturing paid by U.S. trading partners has risen sharply relative to compensation in the United States. Indeed, by 1996 the average production wage across all U.S. trading partners was actually quite close to the average wage of production workers in the United States.[6] This suggests that, even ignor-

6. The wage estimates in figures 4-6 through 4-8 are based on commercial exchange rates, which provide the appropriate basis for comparing nations' trade competitiveness. To compare living standards across countries, however, it is more appropriate to consider the *purchasing power* of each country's average wage. Living standard comparisons are much more favorable to the United States. Because American prices for many nontraded goods and services are significantly lower than they are in other rich countries, average U.S. wages measured using equivalent-purchasing-power exchange rates appear higher than wages measured using commercial exchange rates.

Figure 4-7. Hourly Compensation in Manufacturing, Selected Industrial Countries, 1996

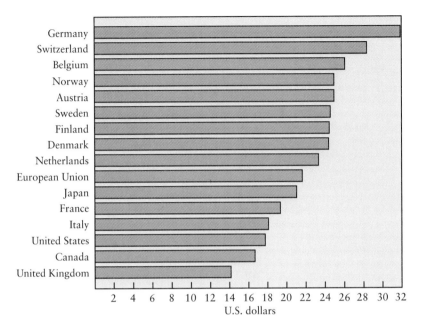

Source: Bureau of Labor Statistics.

Figure 4-8. Hourly Compensation in Overseas Trading Partners as a Share of U.S. Compensation, 1975–96

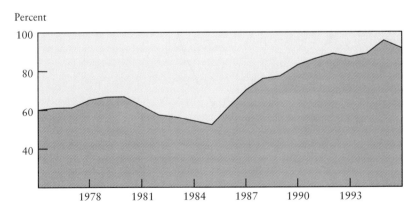

Source: Bureau of Labor Statistics.
a. Estimates of weighted average hourly compensation of production workers in manufacturing among twenty-eight U.S. trading partners (excluding China, where wages are unknown).

ing productivity differences across countries, the average wages of our trading partners cannot be exerting much downward pressure on the average wage in this country.

Fourth, relatively few U.S. workers are in direct competition with Mexican or Chinese workers, or those in other less developed countries. Most American workers produce goods or services for markets in which there is little or no cross-border trade. Retail trade, communications and transportation, health care, construction, and personal services are some of the industries in which U.S. producers exclusively, or almost exclusively, supply U.S. consumers. Poorly paid workers who live in Brazil or China do not compete with U.S. workers in serving restaurant meals, delivering health care, or building homes and office buildings. (However, immigrants from these countries do compete with less skilled native-born workers in the United States and do seem to holding down their wages, as we discuss below.)

Fifth, of those industries in which goods and services do move across international boundaries, there are many in which U.S. and third world workers do not compete directly. One reason is that manufacturing workers in rich and poor countries tend to specialize in making different products. Commercial jets and high-performance computers are manufactured in rich countries; garments and stuffed toys are made in developing countries. Some American workers *are* employed in industries where third world production is important or growing, and they face a serious problem that the nation should address through sensible and humane adjustment assistance of the kind that we detail in our concluding chapter. But it is important to put this issue in perspective. In 1996 the manufacturing sector accounted for just 15 percent of U.S. payroll employment, and most manufacturing jobs were in industries where competition from rich countries is more important than competition from the third world.[7]

Even if low wages in developing countries have not depressed U.S. wages so far, what about the future? After all, it is widely conceded that the populations of these countries, which already dwarf those of more advanced countries, are growing more rapidly than those of the industrialized world. William Greider perhaps expresses best the view that continued population growth and the accompanying expansion of

---

7. Council of Economic Advisers (1997, p. 350).

manufacturing capacity in the developing world will lead to a "global glut" of goods produced by low-wage countries, not only depressing prices around the world, but wages as well.[8]

The notion that third world countries pose a threat to the United States represents a sharp turnaround from the way these countries were viewed during the cold war. Until the demise of the Soviet Union, the developing countries were seen as a battleground for the competing ideologies of capitalism and communism, in some cases to fight with arms, but more commonly with persuasion and propaganda. The United States sought to expand trade with them as a way of making the developing countries richer and convincing them that capitalism—and democracy—held out much more promise for material improvement than central planning and collectivism (and their associated authoritarian political systems).

The U.S. strategy proved successful. Trade has indeed helped to raise average incomes in the developing world, not just absolutely, but also relative to those in the United States. Yet now that capitalist democracies have won the ideological battle, many in the United States seem to have lost faith in the policy of openness that helped produce the victory.

It is time for Americans once again to view the developing world as an enormous economic *opportunity*—that is, a growing and potentially large market for the goods and services that the United States and other rich countries produce—rather than a threat. Since the 1980s, developing country economies have been growing much faster than those of the industrialized world. (Viewed over a span of two decades, this should continue to be true even with the economic slowdown expected in 1998 and possibly future years in Southeast Asia.) Faster growth means not only higher wages, as we have demonstrated, but also increasing consumer demand. The following observations from a September 1997 report issued by the investment house Morgan Stanley Dean Witter provide a powerful illustration of the growth potential for American-made products and services in the developing world:[9]

■ While cellular phones are sweeping the advanced countries and a few emerging markets, more than 50 percent of the world's population has never made a phone call.

8. Greider (1997).
9. Quinlan (1997b).

- Although it may seem that there is a McDonald's on every street corner in the United States, the company still serves only one-half of a percent of the world's population.
- While Fuji and Kodak battle over whether the Japanese market is unfairly closed, half the world's population has never taken a photograph.

Behind each of these nuggets lies a more sweeping fundamental truth. The developing world represents an enormous commercial opportunity for American firms and workers. Given the rapidly declining costs of computing power—and the prospect that televisions and simple "network" devices will bring computing to the masses both here and abroad—the possibilities for American-made products and technology in penetrating markets around the world seems nothing short of mind-boggling.

The critics who raise the specter of global glut overlook the enormous opportunities for the United States and other advanced countries to sell to developing countries. Their claim that developing countries are simply export engines that threaten to overwhelm the world with too many low-priced goods is also flatly wrong. If it were true, one would expect the developing countries to be running large trade surpluses with the rest of the world, in particular, with advanced countries. In fact, as shown in table 4-1 many developing countries have run trade deficits with advanced countries.[10] Moreover, in large areas of the developing world, these deficits had been increasing, not shrinking.

None of this should be surprising. Poor countries do not ship stuffed toys or apparel to the United States out of a sense of charity or with the sinister intent of driving up the U.S. unemployment rate. They expect payment, and with the payments they receive, expect to buy goods and services in international markets. In an efficient world trading system, they would buy products that they could not obtain cheaply from their own producers. It takes little imagination to realize that the advanced countries have much to sell poor countries that they cannot make on their own, or could only produce at higher cost. In short, those who worry about the

---

10. Brazil and Russia are the notable exceptions. Brazil still runs a trade surplus, but this is down sharply in the 1990s compared with the 1980s. And since Russia's capitalism is in its infancy, its businesspeople prefer to keep their hard-currency export earnings abroad rather than spend them on imports, but this situation should change as the economy grows.

TABLE 4-1. Trade Balances with the Industrialized Countries, Selected
Developing Nations, 1980–96
Billions of U.S. dollars

Region and Country	1980–89[a]	1990–96[a]
Asia		
Singapore	−36	−79
Korea	12	−135
Thailand	−17	−56
Malaysia	1	−48
Philippines	−1	−14
Indonesia	63	23
China	−101	−16
India	−33	−5
Pakistan	−16	−7
Latin America		
Argentina	−1	−17
Brazil	72	24
Chile	9	6
Colombia	−2	−6
Mexico	43	−36
Peru	5	−27
Venezuela	19	28
Bolivia	0.1	−1
Ecuador	1	3
Central Europe and former Soviet Union		
Czech Republic[b]	n.a.	−10
Poland	n.a.	−20
Russia[c]	n.a.	58
Hungary	n.a.	−9
Ukraine[c]	n.a.	−5
Estonia[c]	n.a.	−3
Kazakstan[c]	n.a.	−1
Romania[c]	n.a.	−5
Azerbaijan[c]	n.a.	−0.3
Tajikistan[c]	n.a.	0.3
Africa		
Gabon	5	9
Morocco	−11	−14
South Africa	−24	−22

a. Cumulative balance.
b. Data for 1993–96.
c. Data for 1992–96.
Source: International Monetary Fund, *Direction of Trade Statistics Yearbook*, various years.

coming global glut focus only on one side of the economic equation—production—forgetting that more people also means more consumers.

There is another basic reason for the pattern of trade deficits shown in table 4-1. Recall from chapter 2 that trade is simply the flip side of investment. As many developing countries have embraced market institutions, they have attracted increasing flows of capital from around the world. Foreign capital enables poor countries to invest more than they save. When that occurs, they must necessarily import more than they export. People who fear global glut are fundamentally mistaken in charging large capital flows into developing countries with current and future excess global capacity. It is mathematically impossible for countries to be net importers of capital and net exporters of goods. Capital flows into a country are *exactly equal* to that country's excess of imports over exports!

As of this writing, the Asian currency and banking crises that began in the fall of 1997 have already sharply curtailed the flow of foreign capital into those countries, which has contributed to a major decline in their currencies. These changes in exchange rates, in turn, should lead to major shifts in the trade balances of these countries. Yet this does not lend support to fears of a global glut of goods. It only means that, for some period of time, these countries will find it easier to sell their products in international markets, reducing the need for manufacturing capacity elsewhere to expand.

Openness and Rising Inequality

If increased trade is not responsible for the decline in average wages in the United States, surely it must be partly responsible for the increasing *inequality* in incomes over the past two decades.[11] That, after all, seems to be an implication of the Stolper-Samuelson theorem, as well as common sense. Since low-wage workers with few skills overseas are

11. Throughout the industrialized world, income disparities have grown since the early 1980s. However in some European countries, in contrast to the United States, there has been little trend in hourly wage inequality but a sharp increase in joblessness, especially among the young and the least skilled. This increase also contributes to growing social and economic inequality.

in direct competition with less-skilled U.S. workers, does it not follow that this competition must reduce the wages of less-skilled workers relative to those of higher skilled workers in the United States?

That there has been growing inequality in the wages paid to American workers is beyond doubt. A cottage industry has developed within the economics profession in attempting to explain the reasons for this trend. We do not review all of the evidence, much of it highly technical in nature.[12] Rather, we briefly review the relevant trends in greater detail, and then explain in straightforward terms why—as most economists who have studied recent wage developments conclude—trade liberalization accounts for only a small part of the growth of income inequality in the United States.

Recent Trends in Relative Wages

Most Americans recognize that income disparities have grown over the past quarter century, but few may realize the extent of the growth. Consider the broadest unit of comparison: family income. Based on tabulations compiled from Census Bureau surveys, figure 4-9 shows

Figure 4-9. Change in U.S. Real Family Income, 1969–95

Annual percentage change

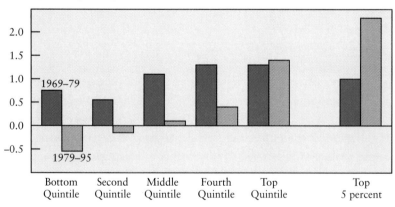

Source: Census Bureau surveys.

12. For excellent summaries of the evidence, see Levy and Murnane (1992), Freeman (1997), and Slaughter and Swagel (1997).

Figure 4-10. Growth in Hourly Real Wages, at Selected Points in U.S. Wage Distribution, by Gender, 1979–96

Annual percentage change

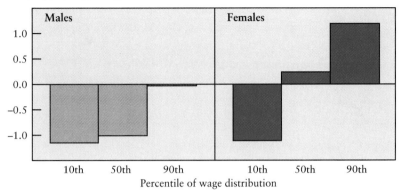

Percentile of wage distribution

Source: Current Population Survey outgoing rotation samples, as estimated by Employment Policy Institute.

the growth rates of income for families in each quintile and also in the top 5 percent of the income distribution, over the periods 1969–79 and 1979–95.[13] The chart shows that income inequality grew in both periods, though it increased much faster in the later period than in the earlier one. Especially disturbing is the fact that incomes in the bottom two quintiles actually fell after 1979 (assuming that the Consumer Price Index is measured reasonably accurately). Average incomes rose in higher quintiles, and in the top 5 percent of the distribution incomes climbed faster than in the decade before 1979.

Figure 4-10 shows that earnings disparities among American workers also have risen, particularly after 1979.[14] The jump in inequality is most striking among men, for whom wages fell in the middle and at the bottom of the distribution and remained roughly unchanged near the top of the distribution. Only men in the top 7 or 8 percent of wage earners enjoyed increases in real hourly pay. The drop in earnings at the bottom of the distribution for men is sub-

13. We pick 1979 as a convenient dividing line because it was a year of relatively full employment, as were 1969 and 1995.
14. Figure 4-11 presents data only on hourly wages because the distributional information for the preferred total compensation measure is not available.

Figure 4-11. Relative Pay of U.S. Workers with Postcollege Education, 1969–95ᵃ

Median earnings ratio[b]

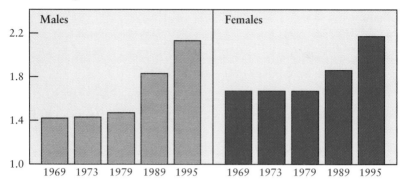

Source: Authors' tabulations from Current Population Surveys for 1970, 1974, 1980, 1990, and 1996 (March files).
a. Data are for full-time, year-round workers.
b. Median pay of workers with postcollege education compared with that of workers who are high school graduates only.

stantial: 18 percent over the period from 1979 to 1996. Furthermore, the figure indicates that although the labor market has in general been kinder to American women, especially at the top of the wage distribution, women at the bottom of the income distribution have fared just as badly as men. There has thus been a sharp increase in inequality among women.

Wage inequality has grown along several dimensions. Older and more experienced workers have seen their wages climb relative to the those of young workers entering the work force. Workers in occupations requiring extensive training have enjoyed more rapid pay increases than those in less-skilled occupations. And perhaps most important, highly educated workers have received much bigger wage hikes than workers with less schooling.

Figure 4-11 shows trends in the relative earnings of the most highly educated group in the labor force—workers with education beyond four years of college—compared to the pay of workers who have completed high school but received no further education. After remaining fairly stable in the 1970s, this ratio soared in the 1980s and 1990s. In 1979 the median male with postcollege education earned 47 percent more than the median male with a high school diploma only. By 1995, the pay differential between these two groups had risen to 113 percent. The earnings premium increased almost as much among women.

Economists sometimes focus only on the impacts that these developments have on people's incomes. But incomes determine families' standard of living in many ways, not only through the goods they purchase, but also in the amount of risk they are exposed to and the quality of health care to which they have access, for example. There is recent evidence that higher inequality is associated with higher death rates, as a result of disease and other causes.[15] Income inequality, therefore, is not just about money; it is about the length and quality of life itself.

Trade and Income Inequality

The changes in wage patterns just described would seem consistent with the theory that low-wage competition from abroad has reduced the relative pay of less-skilled workers. We have shown above that there is reason to be suspicious of this argument, because workers in other countries do not work with the same technologies as U.S. workers, even the lowest paid. There are also other reasons to be skeptical about the impact of trade on income.

If trade were the main factor behind the shrinking demand for—and hence the lower wages of—unskilled workers, firms that did not produce internationally traded goods and services would take advantage of the declining wage by hiring more unskilled workers. If, instead, such firms also decreased their use of unskilled labor, it must be the case that technological change or some other development, rather than trade, is primarily responsible for reducing the demand for less-skilled workers.

To address this question, it is useful to compare wage and employment trends among workers in all U.S. industries and workers in those industries that are highly affected by trade, including manufacturing, mining, and agriculture. Doing so produces the striking result that earnings inequality (calculated as the ratio of annual earnings at the

15. For example, George Kaplan has found a strong correlation between statewide mortality rates and the degree of income inequality among the fifty states; see Koretz (1997).

Figure 4-12. Relative Pay of U.S. Workers without High School Diploma Compared with Pay of U.S. Workers with One to Three Years of College, Trade-Affected and All Industries, 1969–95ᵃ

Percent

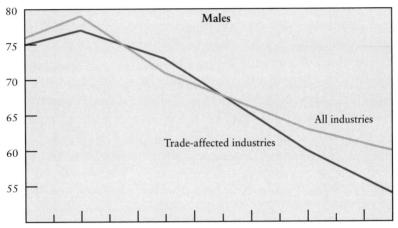

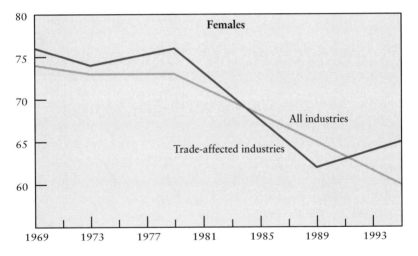

Source: Authors' tabluations from Current Population Surveys for 1970, 1974, 1980, 1990, and 1996 (March files).
a. Data are for full-time workers.
b. Median pay of workers without high school diploma as percentage of median pay of workers with one to three years of college.

ninetieth percentile of the earnings distribution to earnings at the tenth percentile) is growing at about the same rate in the industries that are most affected by trade as in all U.S. industries, including those that are relatively unaffected by trade.

The same pattern of relative earnings changes is apparent in trends among workers with different levels of schooling. Figure 4-12 compares the ratio of the median pay earned by full-time workers without a high school diploma with the pay of those with between one and three years of college education in the industries most affected by trade with this ratio for all industries. The figure shows that the decline in relative pay for workers with little schooling has been about the same in the industries most affected by trade and in all industries—for men, the decline was a little faster in trade-sensitive industries, but for women it was somewhat slower. On the whole, however, there is little evidence that pressure from international trade has contributed to faster growth in wage disparities in the trade-affected industries relative to all industries.

Of course, even if wage inequality and educational pay premiums move in the same direction across different industries, it still may be possible for increased trade to explain some portion of the pronounced shift toward greater inequality. Most economists believe that the U.S. labor market is reasonably competitive and efficient. This means that pay premiums for skill and education should eventually rise and fall together across all industries, whatever the reason for the change. Yet if trade from newly industrializing countries in Asia and Latin America were placing special pressure on producers in trade-affected industries, one would expect these industries to shed low-wage workers more rapidly than industries that faced competitive pressure exclusively from other domestic firms.

Companies in the nontraded sector do not compete with overseas firms, but rather, with other American firms, facing similar hiring costs. Do hiring patterns in the trade-affected and non-trade-affected industries support the expectation that companies in the nontraded sector would take advantage of the relatively lower wages of unskilled American workers? Figure 4-13 shows that they do not. The figure illustrates, for the period 1969–95, the utilization of full-time equivalent workers who have less than a high school diploma in the indus-

Figure 4-13. Percent of Work Force without High School Diploma, Trade-Affected and Non–Trade-Affected Industries, 1969–95

Percent of full-time equivalents

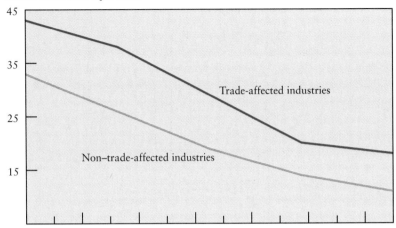

Index, 1969 = 100

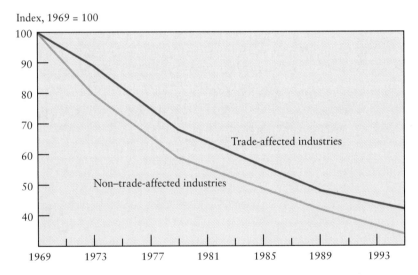

Source: Authors' tabluations from Current Population Surveys for 1970, 1974, 1980, 1990, and 1996 (March files).

tries that are most affected and those that are least affected by trade.[16] The trends in the two classes of industries are clearly quite similar. In particular, the figure suggests that by 1995 the utilization of less skilled workers had fallen 59 percent in the industries most affected by trade and 66 percent in the industries least affected by trade.[17]

In short, figure 4-13 offers little evidence that less-skilled workers have been displaced more rapidly in trade-affected than in non-trade-affected industries (one would reach the same conclusion if educational attainment was divided into narrower schooling categories). If anything, the proportional decline in use of low-skill workers has been slightly faster in the industries that are unaffected by trade than it has been in the trade-affected industries. This pattern of labor use is hard to square with the claim that earnings inequality has been driven mainly, or even significantly, by pressures originating in foreign trade.

If trade is not the main factor in pushing up wage disparities, then what else is? The most plausible explanation, offered by most economists, is that *technological change* has pushed employers throughout the economy to shed less-skilled labor. Over the past quarter of a century, there has been a dramatic shift in the pattern of demand for workers with different levels of skill in the United States. Job opportunities for less-skilled workers have become more scarce, and relative wages for unskilled and semiskilled workers have plunged. These trends are not confined to the traded-goods sector, however. They are also evident in industries, such as construction and retail trade, where international trade plays almost no role. Changes in techniques of pro-

16. A worker who is employed fifty-two weeks in a year on a full-time schedule is a "full-time equivalent" worker. A worker on a part-time schedule employed fifty-two weeks a year is counted as one-half of a full-time equivalent worker, as is a full-time worker who is employed just twenty-six weeks in a year. We have defined "nontrade affected" industries to include construction, retail trade, personal and professional services, and public administration because very little of what is consumed or produced in these industries crosses international borders.

17. Workers in the industries most affected by trade do have somewhat less schooling than other U.S. workers. In 1969, for example, 42 percent of male and 45 percent of female full-time equivalent workers in the trade-affected industries had not completed high school. Over the next twenty-six years, the trade-affected industries slashed the number of less educated workers on their payrolls. By 1995, only 18 percent of male and female workers in these industries lacked a high school diploma. (Authors' calculations based on data from the Current Population Survey.)

duction, such as the invention of the personal computer or the introduction of new forms of business organization, have favored workers with greater skills and reduced the value of unskilled labor.

How can our arguments be reconciled with the Hecksher-Ohlin-Samuelson trade theory, which, as discussed earlier in this chapter, suggests that by depressing the prices of goods that are produced mainly with unskilled workers while raising the prices of export goods made with skilled labor, freer trade should disadvantage low-skilled relative to high skilled workers? Figure 2-8 indicates that since 1980, prices in U.S. export industries have increased faster than imports prices, so there is something to this line of argument. Nonetheless, trade surely is only a small part of the whole story. As this section has shown, technology-driven demand by U.S. employers for skilled labor is probably the dominant factor driving wage inequality in both the trade-sensitive and non-trade-sensitive sectors of the economy. This conclusion is reinforced by the best detailed economic studies, which look beyond simple relationships between export and import prices to focus specifically on the relative prices of products classified by the skill levels of labor required to produce them. These studies fail to find, as the Hecksher-Ohlin-Samuelson theory would suggest, that prices of goods requiring skilled labor have increased at a faster pace than prices of goods relying heavily on unskilled labor.[18] The observed pattern of price changes can easily be explained if technological change has been the driving factor behind both price movements and the shifting demand for different classes of workers.

Other Factors

If trade has not had a significant impact on relative wages in the United States, what about the effects of actual or threatened investment by American firms abroad? For outward foreign direct investment to have been important, it would have to have been substantial and biased

18. See, for example, Lawrence (1996), Lawrence and Slaughter (1993), Sachs and Shatz (1994), and Leamer (1996). Sachs and Shatz find Stolper-Samuelson effects in some of their econometric specifications, but not others. Leamer finds such effects for the 1970s, but not for the 1960s or 1980s.

Figure 4-14. Annual U.S. Investment in Domestic Plant and Equipment and Outward Foreign Direct Investment, 1980 to 1996

Billions of dollars

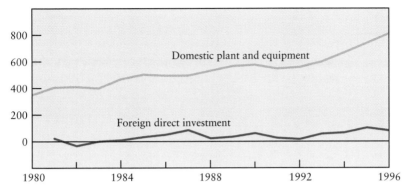

Source: Council of Economic Advisers (1989 and 1997).

heavily toward developing countries whose workers compete most strongly with those in the United States. What are the facts?

Figure 4-14 documents that while U.S. foreign direct investment has been rising over the past two decades, it is dwarfed in magnitude by total investment in plant and equipment in the United States. In 1996, for example, outward foreign direct investment to all countries totaled about $100 billion, compared to about $800 billion of domestic investment in plant and equipment. Moreover, figure 4-15 illustrates that when they do invest in facilities abroad, U.S. sources put most of their money in other developed economies, many of which now pay higher manufacturing wages than the United States, not in developing countries paying low wages. In particular, of the roughly $800 billion in cumulative U.S. direct investment abroad at year-end 1996 (measured at historical cost), about $540 billion had gone to western Europe, Canada, and Japan. Total investment in Mexico—for those who fear the effects of the North American Free Trade Agreement— amounted to only $19 billion, or less than 3 percent of cumulative outward foreign direct investment. As one recent study concludes: "in practice capital flows seem to play a limited role in equalizing productivity across countries . . . international capital flows to poor countries

Figure 4-15. Cumulative U.S. Foreign Direct Investment, by Region or Country, Year-End 1996[a]

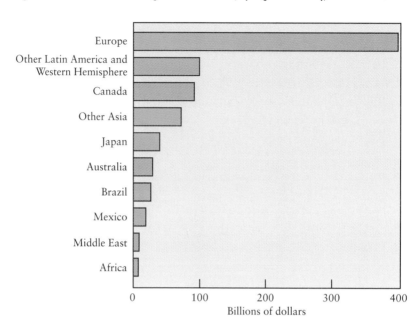

Billions of dollars

Source: Bureau of Economic Analysis.
a. Historical cost basis.

are generally not large enough"[19] to offset the productivity-suppressing effects of low levels of human capital and poor public infrastructure and transportation services.

Nonetheless, there is one factor associated with globalization that clearly does seem to have adversely affected the earnings of low-wage workers in the United States: immigration. The share of the U.S. population that is foreign born has nearly doubled over the past thirty-six years, rising from 5.4 percent in 1960 to 9.3 percent in 1996.

The influx of foreigners, per se, is not the main issue, however. Much more important is the fact that many recent immigrants are far less skilled than other Americans. A recent study suggests that whereas in 1995 less than 12 percent of native-born Americans lacked a high school diploma, 40 percent of legal immigrants into the United States

19. Golub (1997, p. 9).

had not completed a high school education. Furthermore, for the period 1980–95, the influx of immigrants accounted for a 15 to 20 percent increase in the relative supply workers without a high school diploma.[20]

It would be surprising if the law of supply and demand did not work in the labor market. Sure enough, this study estimates that the growth in the supply of low-skilled immigrants between 1980 and 1995 lowered the wages of high school dropouts relative to all other workers by about 5 percent, explaining almost half of the 11 percentage point decline in the wages of these workers over that period. Under the most plausible set of assumptions, however, the growing importance of trade with developing countries is estimated to have accounted for only 8 percent of the relative wage decline of high school dropouts.[21]

Why should the effects of immigration be so different than those of trade, at least for the wages of the least skilled? There are two important reasons. Most important, workers abroad do not have access to the same technologies as do immigrants to the United States. Thus immigrants with equal educational skills can and do directly substitute for a native-born American or earlier immigrants—driving taxis, serving as waiters in restaurants, and working on construction sites—whereas workers abroad cannot serve in these functions. Furthermore, in contrast to trade, which directly affects employment only in the sectors of the economy that compete in internationally traded products, immigrants can and often do displace workers in all sectors of the economy.

The economic evidence on the impact of immigration on the wages of the least-skilled Americans leads to an obvious policy recommendation: in admitting new immigrants, to the extent possible increase the weight given to skills. This is a controversial suggestion, since it necessarily means giving less weight to family ties. But if U.S. voters and

20. Borjas, Freeman, and Katz (1997, p. 4). The educational differences almost certainly would look even larger if all illegal immigrants were included in the analysis.

21. In contrast, neither immigration nor trade have had much impact on the relative wages of high school graduates. These factors have played a very small part (about 5 percent each) in the decline of wages of high school graduates relative to those of college graduates. This is not surprising, either, since only about 40 percent of recent immigrants have been educated beyond the high school level, compared with over 50 percent of native-born Americans.

policymakers are concerned about the drop in absolute and relative wages of the least-skilled, changing the skill mix of admitted immigrants is a concrete step that promises to address the problem.

Summary

While it may seem plausible on the surface, the charge that increased trade and outward foreign investment have depressed *average* wages in the United States is simply not supported by the available hard evidence. There is stronger evidence that liberalized trade has depressed the *relative* wages of less-skilled American workers, although that effect has been relatively small. The wages of less-skilled workers have suffered both relative and absolute declines primarily because employers throughout the economy have shown an increased preference for hiring workers with more advanced skills. It appears that immigration has played an important contributory role in depressing the earnings of the less skilled, and thus in aggravating income inequality, but trade and outward foreign investment have been much less important factors in these developments.

5 FAIRNESS AND LEVEL PLAYING FIELDS

As the century nears its end, America's commitment to open markets and free international trade remains the subject of intense debate. Free trade is essential for a market-based economy to produce the greatest total wealth with a given amount of natural, human, and financial resources. The United States has been successful in encouraging other countries to adopt freer trade policies, forging tighter links between the economies of the world. Developed countries have become interconnected not only through trade, but also through increasing investment flows. Most developing countries have also become more open, seeking both to promote their exports abroad and to reduce barriers to imports and foreign investment.

As globalization proceeds, however, it has become increasingly evident that one nation's economic policies can affect other countries. When nations were separated by high trade barriers and trade flows were limited, one country could ignore another's domestic economic policies. As barriers have come down, other countries' domestic policies have become much more important.

The trade practices of other countries are often described in pejorative terms. For business, the problem is "price dumping," or selling in foreign markets at a price that is below cost or below the price charged in domestic or third country markets. For labor, the problem is "social dumping," or selling goods in the U.S. market at prices that do not reflect the costs of U.S. labor regulations and social safety net programs. And for environmentalists, the problem is "ecodumping," or selling goods in the U.S. market that are produced under less restrictive environmental regulations than the ones that U.S. firms must meet. In all three contexts, the aggrieved parties seek relief from the unwanted foreign competition, either by directly changing the trading rules or by using retaliatory measures or the offer of trade concessions to enforce alternative agreements.

Some people who claim to see deficiencies in other countries' policies are actually seeking a pretext for increased trade protection. Their ultimate goal is not an integrated, rule-based international system, but a fragmented world economy, based on the argument that national differences preclude fair competition.

Others are sincerely committed to freer trade, but are concerned about unfair competition and lax standards for labor practices and environmental issues. They believe that since markets and competition are now global, the rules defining fair competition must also be global. As the world has become aware of shared environmental problems, such as global warming and the depletion of the ozone layer, the case for international coordination of environmental policies becomes stronger. Likewise, as labor markets become linked through trade, and as international humanitarian concerns are heightened by improved publicity and communications (the "CNN effect"), the case for basic universal labor standards has seemed more compelling. In short, for trade to be free, it must first be fair.

Fairness, however, is in the eye of the beholder. What constitutes "fair" and "unfair" has changed over the years.[1] In the 1980s, unfairness was associated with barriers imposed by foreign governments to block market access by U.S. exporters and investors. In addition, unfairness was seen in "industrial policies" that others pursued but the United States did not. Japan was the main target of attack. Authors such as James Fallows, Chalmers Johnson, and Clyde Prestowitz, charged that the decentralized capitalist model governing the U.S. economy was inferior to the Asian or Japanese model, which was mer-

---

1. For excellent guides to the issue of fairness in international trade, see Bhagwati and Hudec (1996) and Krugman (1997b).

cantilist in nature and dedicated to running up large trade surpluses by exporting products, often with state-subsidized credit or other government benefits, while closing the domestic market to foreign competition. In the 1990s one still hears complaints about closed foreign markets, but since the dispute between the United States and Japan over automobiles and parts in 1994 and the meltdown of several Asian economies, the focus of the attack has switched to China, whose state-run economic system is difficult for outsiders to crack and whose political and human rights policies are at odds with some of America's deepest values.

To be fair, not all "fair traders" are alike. Some are willing to take aggressive action; others prefer milder retaliation. However, to focus our discussion of fairness and level playing fields, it is useful to lay out the fair trading argument in its starkest form, without the nuances and qualifications that some of its advocates would include:

The United States' market is free and open, its rules are relatively easy to follow for foreigners and domestic residents alike, and the government provides very little assistance to domestic industries. By contrast, other nations maintain high trade barriers, subsidize their own firms, and discriminate against U.S. producers in many subtle ways. On this playing field, Uncle Sam has become Uncle Sucker. Trade flows are determined not by market forces, but by the policies of other governments. The price Americans pay is evident in the large U.S. trade deficits with some of its most important trading partners. If the United States continues to play by these rules, other countries will use their industrial strategies to nurture and strengthen high-value-added industries—the most desirable industries, those with the highest wages and profits. America will be left with the losers. Even when other countries sign trade agreements, the rules will not cover all their unfair practices. Moreover, other nations cannot be trusted to follow rules that would allow U.S. firms and products to compete fairly. Therefore, the United States should either restrict trade with any economy less open than its own, or pursue its own industrial policies to ensure fair results.

There are three, logically consistent, extreme responses to this call for fair trade. One is to trade only with similar countries, as open as the United States, with similar rules, regulations, wage levels, and labor standards. The second is not to negotiate any more trade deals, thus reversing the trend toward open borders and expanded international agreements and institutions. The third is to pursue aggressive "strategic" industrial and export policies, designed to promote American dominance in high-technology and other critical sectors.

We believe that none of these policies makes sense. It is undesirable for nations either to be completely unconstrained or forced to be alike. With respect to strategic industrial policies, experience in the United States and abroad shows that governments have neither the wisdom nor the freedom from pressure-group politics to make anything but a botch of them.

The appropriate responses are more subtle and nuanced. Abroad, U.S. national interest lies in negotiating international rules and arrangements that lead to open markets, while still leaving wide scope for national autonomy. At home, it is essential to offer compensation and facilitate the adjustment of workers who are harmed by greater openness. The ideal is balanced global and national rules, and also openness and diversity, while combining the efficiency benefits of free trade with an equitable distribution of the costs of adjustment.[2] We make this case in the rest of the book, beginning in this chapter by demonstrating that freer trade is beneficial even if it is not carried out on a level playing field.

The Virtues of Difference

At one level, the fairness argument runs both ways. While many Americans believe that foreigners practice unfair trade because of their low wages and distortionary government policies, many foreigners have an equally hostile view of American policies and institutions. They complain, for example, about the benefits enjoyed by many

---

2. For a more extensive discussion, see Lawrence, Bressand, and Ito (1996).

domestic producers as a result of U.S. defense spending, and they often express horror at the complexity and expense of the U.S. legal and regulatory system.

Nonetheless, there is a superficial plausibility to the claim that one is bound to lose in international competition if others appear to have advantages. After all, it is hard to win a one-hundred-yard dash if one's opponent starts fifty yards closer to the finish line. But the sports metaphor is fundamentally misleading. Sports games are zero-sum contests, with distinct winners and losers. But when two nations trade, both profit from the exchange. As long as foreign producers sell Americans goods more cheaply than they can be made at home, the United States will gain, regardless of whether the producers' markets or open or closed. As noted in chapter 2, it makes no sense to erect barriers to trade simply because others maintain them—one only ends up paying higher prices than necessary.[3]

More fundamentally, the earlier discussion demonstrated that many of the gains from trade are due precisely to the fact that the playing field is *not* level. Trade benefits both partners because national environments—including natural resources and technology, as well as government policies—*are different*. The explanation of trade in terms of technology and relative factor endowments is so commonly accepted that the discovery that comparative advantage can actually be influenced (or created) by government action is sometimes considered a major refutation of that principle. Yet David Ricardo, who first derived the law of comparative advantage, might as well have attributed productive differences between nations to the social climate as to the physical climate; his conclusions about the benefits of eliminating trade barriers would have been the same. As long as government rules and spending legitimately reflect local conditions and preferences, free trade will achieve a globally efficient distribution of resources. Indeed, the more different are the standards and costs of a nation's trading partners, the greater will be that nation's gains from trading with them.

3. In theory, a large country can improve its welfare through protection if it can alter the terms of trade in its favor; for example, by using its market power as a large buyer to force other countries to sell their goods at much lower prices than they would do otherwise. However, this result—known as the optimal tariff argument—depends on other countries not retaliating in kind.

If national tastes, conditions, or incomes lead to different laws, the playing field of international competition will not—and should not—be level.[4] It should be clear, therefore, that international competition between firms based in different economies is unlikely to be fair in the same way as competition between firms within an economy. Proposals such as tariffs on imported products to offset lower production costs abroad, not only would level the playing field, as intended, but would nullify the gains from trade. Traditional determinants of costs, such as relative factor endowments, technology, and taste should affect trade performance, and so also should regulations, institutions, and government policies. This is true of the domestic economy, in which the states implement different tax policies, have different wage levels, and maintain different labor and environmental rules, and yet trade between them continues.

There is need for a basic legal infrastructure that allows all players to be confident that their payments will be accepted and rights to their property, physical and intangible, will be enforced. But again, the laws do not need to be identical: within the United States, for example, laws governing contracts, property, and torts, are administered by the fifty states and differ among them. The rules just need to meet some minimum standard of protection and be clear enough for everyone to understand.

Not all groups in a country will benefit from the different rules and standards in its trading partners. If a nation maintains relatively lenient pollution standards, at least two groups might object: producers of pollution-intensive products in other nations with stricter standards and advocates of a clean environment in the nation with lax standards. But as long as standards reflect the outcome of a legitimate political process in each nation, the outcome should improve aggregate welfare, both at home and abroad. The countries with tougher pollution standards will get what they want: less pollution. The country with lenient standards will get what it wants: more output from pollution-intensive industries.

To be sure, this "live and let live" approach is only appropriate for pollution that does not cross national borders. When emissions from

4. See Bhagwati and Srinivasan (1996).

one country can harm the environment of others, other countries policies do make a difference. This so-called externalities problem is the reason why many countries have agreed on a global approach to stopping and ideally reversing the depletion of the earth's ozone layer, with the result that substantial reductions in fluorocarbon emissions have occurred. The December 12, 1997, Kyoto agreement on targets for greenhouse gases, which are widely believed to contribute to global warming, was made in the same spirit—although reasonable people can and do differ about the merits of this latter agreement.

In sum, free trade and national sovereignty need not be inconsistent. In fact, together they provide the basic principles for operating a nation state in a global economy.

Agreeing to Trade

The case for unilateral free trade rests on the assumption that nations do not have influence over the behavior of their trading partners. Yet as discussed in chapter 2, much of the liberalization of the world economy has taken place as a result of international negotiations. There are many reasons why it can be in a nation's interest to enter into such agreements, rather than to pursue unilateral free trade.

First, even though a nation may benefit from removing its own barriers to trade, it can do even better if its trading partners also eliminate their barriers, raising the demand for the nation's exports and thus improving its buying power in international markets. If a nation can use the carrot of lowering its own barriers to induce another nation to do the same, both nations benefit. Reciprocity of some kind may be desirable, not because it is in some sense "fair," but because it may be more effective in achieving mutually beneficial trade.

Second, international negotiations can strengthen the influence of those who gain from free trade. While trade may be in the national interest, it creates some losers in the industries that compete with imports. If the losers are politically powerful, they may block a unilateral reduction in barriers. Trade negotiations might mobilize one group of domestic producers—exporters who would gain from liberalization abroad—to offset the influence of those domestic producers and workers who would compete with the imports, and thus make it politically easier for leaders to adopt policies in the nation's interest.

Third, international agreements can give a nation's liberal trade policies greater credibility. Before firms will undertake the investments needed to serve foreign markets, they need to be confident that access to these markets will be forthcoming. When countries, particularly those with a long history of protection, proclaim a new-found allegiance to open trade and investment, investors often react quite skeptically. By undertaking commitments that can provoke international sanctions if they are broken, countries can persuade others of the permanence of their changes. As discussed in chapter 3, this "lock-in" motive was a principal reason why President Salinas wanted Mexico to join the North American Free Trade Agreement (NAFTA). The United States and Canada agreed with this strategy.

Fourth, international agreements can also prove useful when international markets deviate significantly from the competitive model implicitly assumed by Ricardo's law of comparative advantage. One such market failure occurs when firms have monopoly or market power, that is, have the ability to set prices rather than being forced to accept those determined by the forces of supply and demand. Countries that adopt policies to enhance the market power of their firms—so-called strategic trade policies—seek to exploit this market imperfection to boost the prices of their exports in world markets at the expense of other nations. International rules or oversight that inhibit such behavior could, in principle, improve global welfare. Similarly, as noted above, international agreements can be necessary to address "spillovers," such as cross-border pollution, and may be useful for setting common standards. The benefits of harmonizing standards may involve a trade-off, however. On the one hand, local regulations may match specific preferences more closely; on the other, international norms may yield benefits from scale economies.

All of these considerations were reflected in the most recent successful multilateral trade negotiation, the Uruguay Round of the General Agreement on Tariffs and Trade (GATT), which created the World Trade Organization (WTO). Under this agreement, 125 nations not only committed themselves to a series of tariff reductions, but also agreed to continue bargaining multilaterally to reduce other trade barriers, such as those dealing with services and government procurement. To ensure that these negotiations are credible, WTO members have consented to an international tribunal that will impose sanctions in the event that an individual nation reneges on its commitments. And to prevent the reductions in trade barriers from being undermined by domestic policies, WTO members also have agreed to avoid measures that discriminate against foreign goods and to frame new domestic policies so that, to the extent possible, they achieve their goals in the manner least restricting to trade.

Nonetheless, while the WTO system is based on the principles of nondiscrimination between members ("most favored nation treatment") and nondiscrimination between domestic and imported goods ("national treatment"), it does not require that nations maintain tariffs at identical levels or adopt identical domestic policies. Even with respect to border barriers, the Uruguay Round agreement does not require a level playing field. While it does expressly prohibit export subsidies, GATT only allows nations to respond to foreign subsidies and dumping when these are determined to cause injury. In short, the goal of multilateral negotiation through GATT has not been to create a level playing field, but instead to allow the benefits of international specialization to be more fully realized.

Does the United States Lose on the International Playing Field?

So much for principles, but what about practice? What should one make of claims that the United States has suffered because it has liberalized more than its trading partners? How should one evaluate proposals to move toward more protectionist and interventionist policies to help our domestic producers?

The United States may be more open than most countries, but some have recently come a long way toward trade liberalization, having begun the postwar period with higher barriers than the United States. As noted earlier, the United States reduced its tariffs by smaller margins than other parties to the Uruguay Round agreement; and similarly, by a smaller margin than Mexico under NAFTA. Meanwhile, a growing number of nations are moving toward free trade and investment with their neighbors. In 1994, leaders from eighteen extremely diverse countries around the Pacific Rim assembled in Indonesia and pledged to achieve mutual free trade and investment by 2020. In the same year in Miami, thirty-four nations of the Western Hemisphere agreed to conclude negotiations for hemispheric free trade by 2005.[5] These initiatives provide clear evidence that the principles of freer trade and markets are gaining worldwide acceptance. Given the United States' critical role in making that case, and in view of the benefits that it stands to enjoy as overseas markets become more open, it has good reason to applaud this development.

Some foreign countries, particularly those in the early stages of development, do adopt industrial policies that enhance the competitive positions of favored groups of their own firms—as Alexander Hamilton succeeded in arranging for America in its early years. Nonetheless, since World War II, the United States has remained extremely competitive by means of maintaining open markets. While economic theory can show that, under certain conditions, a government can improve national welfare through strategic trade policies favoring selected domestic industries, theory also suggests that the conditions under which that success will occur are not likely to be realized in practice. In contrast to nineteenth-century America, with infant industries, such as steam engines and machine tools, whose economic value was well established in Europe's more advanced economies, today's government would have to predict the particular industries and firms that would lead technological development at some time in the future.

In theory, trade protection might promote the development of infant industries, the promotion of some high-technology industries might produce external benefits for the rest of society, and strategic trade subsidies might shift market "rents" (higher than normal profits) between countries. But in the real world, what bureaucrat knows enough to pick which industries are suitable infants for protection or subsidy, and where to uncover the rents in international markets? And what politician can be trusted to grant such favors—or to end them

---

5. APEC (1994); and "Summit of the Americas Declaration of Principles" (World Wide Web).

when appropriate—free from the influence of special interests? Only impersonal markets have the capacity to perform these functions, and they sometimes do so by letting many firms fail.

In fact, the most successful and innovative industries in the U.S. economy of the 1990s, such as software and financial services, have prospered without any trade protection or subsidies. Moreover, in these and other leading-edge industries—aircraft, bioengineering, telecommunications, pharmaceuticals, chemicals, and entertainment—American firms are the envy of the world. At the same time, in other countries, including Japan, critics of industrial policy question whether extensive regulatory control and interventionist government policies are appropriate for nurturing industrial competitiveness. South Korea, Thailand, and Indonesia for years used their banking systems to channel funds to favored firms and industries, only to discover in 1997 that this policy had led to massive overinvestment in commercial property and excess manufacturing capacity, which brought these countries to the edge of bankruptcy. (They were rescued by the International Monetary Fund under the condition that they fundamentally reform their banking systems.)

Even in theory, strategic policy could apply only to a handful of industries with two or three worldwide producers. As noted above, it could backfire if governments in competitor countries responded by subsidizing their own producers. Furthermore, by lulling beneficiary companies into complacency, subsidies unwittingly open the door for firms in third countries to wrest market share from these favored firms. In the 1980s, industrial policy and strategic trade policy were widely touted as a means of boosting U.S. economic performance. Not much is heard about these policies now. One possible reason is that in the drive to balance the budget, there has been little room for using tax credits or discretionary spending to promote particular private sector activities.[6] Another reason is that strong American economic perfor-

---

6. The closest approximation to an "industrial policy" has been the Clinton administration's Advanced Technology Program (ATP), administered by the Commerce Department, which awards matching grants to developers of certain "generic" technologies. The administration argued that by requiring that recipients contribute half of the research and development costs themselves, the government was not picking winners, but rather, selecting among winners already chosen by the market. The Republican-controlled Congress attempted to kill the ATP during Clinton's first term, but succeeded only in scaling back its size.

mance during the 1990s has made the notion of special aid to particular industries seem antiquated and unnecessary.

In any event, the American system of government—with its checks
and balances, its inherent mistrust of bureaucratic discretion in particular and government in general, and its relative openness to the plead-
ings of special interests—makes the United States especially ill suited to
a regime of expensive industrial policy or managed trade. U.S. firms
may not always perform well in competition with those from other
nations, but why would one want to substitute the present system for
one in which U.S. bureaucrats compete with overseas bureaucrats?

More broadly, concern about unlevel playing fields for American
firms is somewhat less evident in the 1990s than it was in the 1980s.
Fair traders are now focusing their attention less on other developed
countries than on developing nations, such as China, which have not
yet fully conformed to the basic disciplines of the international trading system. With numerous state-owned companies maintained by
state subsidies and loans, inhibitions about private transactions, its
willingness to use the carrot of a large market to compel the transfer
of technology, and its failure to enforce intellectual property and
labor rights, China presents a host of challenges to U.S. policymakers.
The United States should not give up in the face of this challenge.
The solution is to persuade China to join the WTO, and to insist that
in doing so it meets the conditions and rules that membership currently requires.

On the other side, the United States is hardly an innocent and dis-
advantaged victim of the foreign trade policies of other nations. The
United States has been quite willing to use the threat of closing its
enormous market to try to change foreign practices that it views as
unfair. Under section 301 of the Trade Act of 1974, the president not
only can enforce U.S. rights under international trade agreements, but
also can respond to actions that "burden U.S. commerce." Section 301
and follow-up amendments to "super" and "special" 301 have been
invoked frequently since 1974.[7] While many of these initiatives have
been concluded to the U.S. government's satisfaction, other nations
have bitterly criticized section 301 as a unilateral weapon that can tar-

7. Bayard and Elliott (1994).

TABLE 5-1. Disputes Mediated by the World Trade Organization since Its Creation

| | Respondents | | | |
Complainants	United States	Developed countries	Developing countries	Total filed
United States	n.a.	12	8	20
Developed countries	4	6	7	17
Developing countries	7	3	6	16
Multiple countries	0	1ª	1ª	2ª

Source: World Trade Organization, *Annual Report*, various issues.
a. United States was cocomplainant.

get other countries unfairly, such as when the law is used to deal with foreign practices that have not been the subject of international agreement. When the United States brings action under section 301, it is not only the complainant, but the judge and the executioner as well!

Partly in an effort to persuade the United States to rely on multilateral approaches to settle its disputes, the WTO has adopted a much tougher dispute settlement mechanism. Table 5-1 shows that to date the United States has been the most active complainant under this system and has won a variety of important cases, including matters involving Japan's taxes on liquor imports and its failure to provide adequate protection of the intellectual property represented by American sound recordings. The United States lost a preliminary WTO ruling in late 1997, arguing in behalf of Kodak that the Japanese market is artificially closed to its film. But overall, the WTO has supported U.S. interests: in the fourteen prior cases brought by the United States, the WTO either ruled entirely in favor of the United States or arranged that the target of the complaint make favorable concessions.[8]

Nor is the United States defenseless against foreign exporters whom it deems to behave unfairly.[9] Antidumping laws provide protection to domestic producers from injurious foreign sales, made at "less than fair value" or subsidized by foreign governments. Yet, as outlined in

8. Greenberger, Johannes, and Kerber (1997, p. A14).
9. Robert Shapiro does not join the views expressed about antidumping laws in this paragraph and the accompanying box.

Dumping: Unfair to Whom?

Since it is hard to define unfairness, it is no surprise that efforts to combat it have been poorly designed and at times counterproductive. A prime example is U.S. antidumping law, which is repeatedly defended as a method of addressing unfairness, but in fact contains important elements that are grossly unfair to foreign producers.

Under current rules, dumping is defined either as "price discrimination" (selling export products at prices below those charged at home or, if sales at home are insufficient, below prices charged in third countries) or selling below "fair value" (defined below). In either case, if such practices result in "material injury"—in practice, a relatively small adverse impact—to domestic firms, an offsetting duty in the amount of the "dumping margin" is applied.

What is unfair about the forbidden pricing practices? Consider the first definition of dumping: selling at lower prices in the foreign market. Because foreign producers often must set their prices for foreign customers in terms of foreign currency, fluctuations in exchange rates can cause them to "dump," as defined here. For example, when their home currency appreciates, it takes fewer units of their currency to buy a dollar. But if foreign exporters are meeting the competition in the United States and setting their prices in dollars, the appreciation of their currency will cause the price of their exports in terms of their home currency to fall, making it appear that they are dumping in this market. Under the U.S. antidumping law, domestic American firms are not required to meet the standard imposed on foreign firms selling in the United States. Is the antidumping law redressing an unfairness—or creating one?

Totally apart from exchange rate movements, foreign producers may sell at lower prices abroad than at home because they have market power at home. But what is unfair about that? If anything, it should be the consumers in the producer's home market who complain about unfairly high prices, not other countries that benefit from buying the same products at lower prices. The antidumping rules, however, are not aimed at protecting U.S. consumers, but the U.S. producers who may compete with foreign exporters. The foreign producers may have market power abroad because of artificial barriers to competition set up by their own governments. But if that is the case, the solution is to negotiate away those barriers, not to penalize U.S. consumers through antidumping laws.

The second definition of dumping—selling at less than fair value—makes even less sense. Fair value, under the anti-dumping law, is equated with average costs plus an allowance for profit. Before 1995, when the law was changed pursuant to the Uruguay Round agreement, a profit rate of 8 percent was automatically added to the calculation of cost. Under current law, the actual profit rate is used. Yet economic theory suggests that under competitive conditions, firms price their goods at *marginal* costs, which are often below average costs. As a result, the antidumping laws punish firms that are simply acting in a manner typical of competitive markets. And the law is already unfair, because U.S. firms selling at home are not subject to the same rules. Indeed, it is quite possible for a foreign firm that is selling at a loss both at home and in the United States to be found guilty of dumping, when U.S. firms are also making losses and selling in the domestic market at exactly the same price!

the accompanying box, U.S. antidumping rules have several features that heavily favor domestic producers to the detriment of their foreign competitors. Unfortunately, this antidumping "technology" has become one of the nation's leading policy exports. Under the mantle of addressing "unfairness," an increasing number of countries around the world are now also resorting to antidumping rules as an instrument of trade protection.

In sum, there is a case for international agreements to liberalize trade with countries whose policies are different from those of the United States. Removing foreign barriers to trade makes the U.S. economy more efficient by enabling American firms to sell more of what they have a comparative advantage in producing. Meanwhile, although the playing field will never be level (nor should it be), international rules of the game can ensure that markets remain open even as individual nations express their characters through their different legal systems and national policies.

Unfair Trade and the Trade Balance

Perhaps one of the most widespread mistaken notions about foreign trade is that the trade balance reflects whether countries have open or closed markets. In reality, however, countries with closed markets—such as Mexico in the early 1980s and some of the Southeast Asian countries embroiled in the recent Asian currency and banking crisis—have run large trade deficits. And countries with open markets—such as West Germany, before unification—have run large trade surpluses.

If the openness of the economy does not determine a nation's trade balance, what does? In simple terms: spending patterns. Japan has had a large trade surplus (at least for the past twenty years) because it has been spending less than its income. Indeed, while the Japanese economy has been in recession or stagnating, its imports have plummeted, contributing to an increase in its trade surplus. Suppose that Japan found a way to increase its domestic spending, in the process eliminating its trade deficit. That would not suddenly mean that its market was more open.

Conversely, suppose that Japan opened its markets further, as U.S. trade negotiators have been advocating for decades. Would that lead to a reduction in its overall trade surplus? Perhaps for a time, as imports rose. But as they did so, the Japanese currency would decline in value relative to others. This would make Japanese exports cheaper in terms of those other currencies, so that its exports would increase, eventually essentially offsetting any increase in its imports and restoring the trade balance to its original level. This process would take place, albeit more slowly, even if Japan's exchange rate were fixed. More imports would hold down the rate of price inflation in Japan, over time helping to make Japanese exports more competitive with goods sold from other countries.

In short, the trade balance is not fundamentally affected by trade policy—that is, whether and to what extent the United States and other countries practice "fair trade." It is, instead, a consequence of macroeconomic activity.[10] If a country produces more than it consumes at home, it must, by definition, run a positive trade balance (surplus). Conversely, if a nation consumes more than it produces, then it must be running a trade deficit.

As discussed in chapter 2, to finance a trade deficit, a country must borrow from abroad or cover the deficit with other income flows, such as dividends and interest earned abroad. The "current account" sums activity in both the trade account and these other sources of foreign income and payments. If a country has a positive current account, then it is spending less than its total income and lending the difference to the rest of the world. Conversely, running a current account deficit requires a nation to borrow from the rest of the world, or alternatively, to sell some of its domestically owned assets to foreigners.

The United States would not need to borrow abroad if neither of its two major sectors—the government and the private sector—had to borrow, or if net saving by one more than offset borrowing by the other. Whether government (at all levels) needs to borrow depends on whether taxes cover spending. If taxes exceed government spending, the government is saving; if taxes fall short of spending, the government runs a deficit, and is said to be dissaving. Likewise, whether the

10. This discussion of the U.S. trade and current account balances draws heavily on the explanation provided by the Council of Economic Advisers (1996, pp. 250–51).

private sector needs to borrow is determined by whether private investment exceeds private saving. If businesses and households save less than they invest, they must borrow from the government surplus or from foreigners to finance the excess.

Thus by definition, a nation's balance on its current account will equal the sum of net government borrowing and private sector borrowing; or even more simply, *the difference between national saving and investment.* Countries that save through the government and the private sector more than they invest, as does Japan, run current account surpluses. Countries that invest more than they save at home, as the United States has done for more than two decades, must run current account deficits. Unfairness has nothing to do with it.

This is not to say that the current account is determined entirely by domestic factors, or that "causation" only runs from domestic saving and investment to the trade account. The total investment in a country, for example, can be strongly influenced by how much capital foreigners wish to bring in from abroad. Countries that offer high or exceptionally safe returns to investors will attract capital. Primarily for that reason, some countries run current account deficits for decades: investment (from both foreign and domestic sources) simply exceeds domestic saving. But the essential point remains: the balance of "unfairness" in the world has virtually no impact on the long-run balance of trade.

Figure 5-1 illustrates the U.S. current account deficit and the federal budget deficit during the postwar period. As can be seen, from the early 1970s up to 1987 there was a close positive relationship between the two deficits. The discussion above should help to make clear why this could be so. If the U.S. government had to borrow in such large volume that its requirements swamped the net saving of the private sector, by definition, the country was forced to run a deficit on its current account.

But figure 5-1 also shows that the strong positive relationship between the current account and the federal budget deficit has disappeared over the past decade. Indeed, the two measures seem to have been inversely related since 1987. Does this mean that the fundamental identity between the current account and the national saving-investment balance has been proven wrong? The answer is no,

Figure 5-1. Budget and Current Account Deficits as Shares of GDP, 1959 to mid-1990s

Percent of GDP[a]

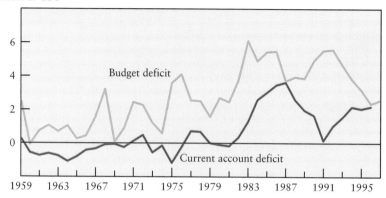

Source: *Historical Tables: Budget of the U.S. Government, Fiscal Year 1998;* Council of Economic Advisers (1997).
a. Negative values indicate a surplus.

for a simple reason: the current account is determined by net borrowing by the private sector, as well as by the government. Figure 5-2 displays government borrowing, private sector borrowing, and the current account, each expressed as a share of total output. The chart indicates that while total government borrowing was rising in the late 1980s and early 1990s, the private sector had become a net

Figure 5-2. Public and Private Sector Saving or Borrowing and the Current Account as a Share of GDP, 1959–96

Percent of GDP

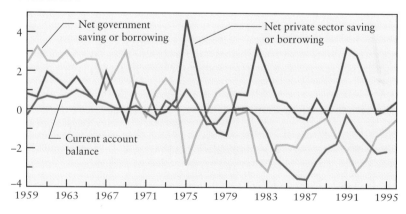

Source: Council of Economic Advisers (1997).

saver, which explains why the current account deficit dropped sharply. Since 1992, the government deficit and its borrowing have dropped, but the current account deficit has risen again. This is the result of faster growth in investment than saving in the private sector (where net saving has essentially vanished). In short, national income accounting is alive and well, and continues to confirm that the nation's current account and trade performance reflects the operation of macroeconomic forces, not the fairness of trade.

Claims that the Asian crisis will lead to a much larger U.S. trade deficit in 1998 (and perhaps beyond) also do not contradict the conventional explanation that links our trade performance with savings and investment behavior. First, it is important to recognize that the trade deficit would have been large (and possibly growing) anyhow—even had the Asian troubles not occurred—as long as the economy continues to grow and investment growth continues to outpace the growth of national saving (as has been true for the past several years and, at this writing, is widely projected to occur this year). Second, some significant share of any increased imports from Southeast Asia (resulting from the depreciation of currencies in that region relative to the dollar) will displace goods that the United States otherwise would have imported from other countries, such as those from Latin America and China. One therefore cannot assume that all of the growth of imports from Asia will add dollar-for-dollar to the trade deficit.

It is nonetheless likely that the problems in Asia will enlarge the trade deficit somewhat because the availability of significantly cheaper Asian imports may induce American consumers and businesses to buy more goods than they otherwise would. To this degree, then, events abroad can affect our own saving and investment patterns. But these impacts will be temporary. In the case of Asia, our larger trade deficits eventually will lead to a weaker dollar, a result that will be reinforced as economies abroad recover and some of the "flight capital" that has found a safe haven in the dollar returns to those countries. As this occurs, U.S. exports will strengthen and imports will be dampened.

If trade barriers do not have any more than temporary effects on the nation's trade balance, why should the United States fight to bring them down? The main reason is that the ultimate goal of national economic policy is to improve the nation's well-being, not to achieve a particular trade balance. Other things equal, it is better for the value of a nation's currency to be high than low. A stronger dollar gives Americans more purchasing power in buying foreign-made goods and services. If the removal of foreign barriers strengthens the value of the dollar, then it improves Americans' standard of living, regardless of the long-term effect on the trade balance. For that reason, elimination of foreign trade barriers is beneficial to the United States. Indeed, in general, the more barriers to trade are removed, the more trade there will be worldwide. And since trade is a critical channel for promoting specialization, the higher the level of trade, the greater will be the benefits to consumers, in each country and around the world.

The primacy of macroeconomic factors in determining the trade balance exposes fundamental flaws in some of the "remedies" that trade critics have advanced for dealing with the U.S. trade deficit. Some trade critics have urged the United States to penalize all countries that practice social dumping (presumably, all countries with lower wages than ours) with an offsetting tariff. Lester Thurow (certainly no globaphobe), urges a policy of retaliatory subsidies under which the United States would announce its readiness to match foreign subsidies dollar for dollar.[11]

There are two problems with these policies. First, they presume that other countries would not retaliate against the United States. This may or may not be correct, but certainly one cannot be totally confident of it. Second, and more fundamentally, to the extent that the aim of social or penalty tariffs is to correct either the total or the bilateral trade deficit, macroeconomic forces will act against it. Higher tariffs in the United States will simply drive up the value of the dollar relative to the currencies of the affected countries. A stronger dollar will make U.S. exports less competitive abroad, thus eventually offsetting any improvement to the trade balance from the reduction in imports. Thurow's proposed retaliatory subsidies would have the same effect, helping the exports of the firms benefiting from the subsidies but hurting the export opportunities of all other firms forced to compete under the handicap of a somewhat strengthened dollar.

11. Thurow (1992).

In short, those who would impose higher trade barriers against foreign countries in the misguided hope of bringing the U.S. trade account into balance, like King Canute shouting at the waves, will inevitably fail in the face of the macroeconomic factors—the balance of national saving and investment—that determine the levels of the trade and current accounts.

CHAPTER

6 OPENNESS, SOVEREIGNTY, AND STANDARDS

hereas in the 1980s trade critics focused on the specter of
unlevel playing fields, in the 1990s the attack on global
integration has become much more far-reaching. One such
criticism is that globalization, by its very nature, under-
mines national self-rule. Citizens vote for governments that pledge to
carry out particular policies, but when international capital markets
deem them inappropriate, financial crisis looms if the policies are
implemented. Citizens may demand social programs that provide
health care and retirement income, macroeconomic policies that maintain high employment, regulations that protect consumers and workers, or a progressive tax system. But once foreign trade and investment
are free to cross international borders, world financial markets can
generate economic pressures that override these democratically determined demands. James Carville, then one of President Clinton's political advisors, was so impressed by this power that he remarked early
in the administration's first term, "[In the next life,] I want to come
back as the bond market."[1]

A related criticism is that globalization allows firms to detach themselves from their national moorings and move to distant shores at the
slightest provocation. Nervous at this prospect, national governments

1. Woodward (1994, p. 145).

therefore refrain from taking steps that would impose basic social responsibilities on major companies. In a closed economy, a society can, through its government, force firms to pay a minimum wage, provide retirement and health benefits, and meet tough environmental standards. But in a borderless global economy, it is claimed, investment will flow out of those nations that impose tough standards and into countries that do not require businesses to accept such responsibilities. Likewise, governments might cut taxes on businesses in order to keep them from relocating abroad. In short, these critics complain that global integration limits a society's ability to finance social progress and distribute income more equitably.

The new World Trade Organization (WTO), established under the General Agreement on Tariffs and Trade (GATT) in 1994 to settle trade-related disagreements, has attracted a different set of criticisms. The United States was a principal supporter of the creation of the WTO, having been dissatisfied with the earlier resolution process administered by the GATT, which required a unanimous decision by the panels selected to hear trade-related cases. This unanimity principle allowed one or two dissenting representatives to prevent a resolution favorable to the United States. In contrast, under the auspices of the WTO, panels decide on cases by majority vote, which has enabled the United States to prevail in more disputes than in the past. Indeed, it now takes unanimity to prevent the WTO from hearing cases or adopting decisions.

An unusual alliance of interests nevertheless has attacked the WTO for usurping sovereignty that belongs to the United States. From the left come charges that the WTO can nullify environmental, labor, and other regulations adopted in the United States if it judges them to be impediments to trade. A closely related criticism was leveled against the North American Free Trade Agreement (NAFTA) and its side agreements, under which the United States consented to give trinational panels the authority to oversee its administration of certain trade, environmental, and labor standards. The American right has attacked international bodies such as the WTO for claiming powers that it believes belong to the U.S. government at all its levels. The transfer of power to international organizations, it is argued, shifts decisionmaking authority from local arenas to unresponsive tribunals on distant shores. These charges find a receptive audience among Americans who may not be familiar with the WTO and how international trade disputes are handled.

Finally, critics of global integration have fiercely attacked recent trade deals for ignoring standards governing working conditions and environmental quality and overlooking some nations' blatant disregard of fundamental human rights. Those critics who accept the legitimacy of the WTO want that organization to enforce tough labor, environmental, and human rights standards as part of the trade agreements themselves. Other critics, who object to the participation of the United States in the WTO, suggest a different policy: The United States should limit access to its market to countries whose behavior accords with its own values. It should use trade sanctions to induce other nations to respect basic rights, a policy that the United States has pursued in relation to Cuba and South Africa. According to this view, the American government should not allow its commitment to open trade to enrich nations whose behavior it rightly deplores.

Most of these criticisms are misplaced. In this chapter we explain why.

Sovereignty and Global Markets

The concern that global integration threatens national sovereignty is based on a basic misunderstanding of how international markets work. World capital markets provide nations with *more options*, not fewer. If nations were forced always to pay cash for a purchase, they would not be burdened with debt, but they would be much more constrained in their purchases of goods and services. Nations that prefer to buy now and pay later—to invest more than they save—are better off if they can borrow. To be sure, if they borrow more than they can afford to repay, they may face painful constraints from their creditors and be forced to retrench. But it is not the ability to borrow that limits a nation's choices; rather, it is the decision to borrow too much, to use credit unwisely by consuming rather than investing it, or, as the events in southeast Asia attest, to invest in projects with low, or even negative, returns.

Political conservatives sometimes invoke globalization as a reason for curtailing social welfare spending that they dislike. They argue, for example, that generous retirement benefits will make U.S. producers uncompetitive in world markets and are thus unwise. In fact, however, the government of a competitive and productive open economy can create public programs that provide its citizens with substantial health, retirement, welfare, and other benefits—so long as its citizens value and are willing to pay for those benefits. Imagine two countries, in which the generosity of public health insurance benefits differs significantly. In one country (say, Canada) health protection is guaranteed to all citizens and financed through taxes. In the other (say, the United States) workers must purchase health care without public subsidies or obtain insurance through voluntary private health plans. At first glance, it may seem that the country that guarantees generous health benefits must be less competitive because of the high social cost of ensuring that all citizens have access to a minimum package of benefits. Firms and workers in Canada are apparently at a cost disadvantage relative to workers and firms in the United States, where citizens are not covered by public health insurance.

For two reasons, however, the generous public health insurance plan has no impact on the competitiveness of Canadian workers and firms. First, if the insurance protection is valued by workers, one would expect other components of compensation to be adjusted to meet the extra cost of health insurance. Total compensation per hour is not necessarily high because health insurance is a mandatory component. Second, even if Canadian labor compensation is increased as a result of the generous health protection available to Canadian citizens, there is no reason to expect that Canadian labor compensation, measured in U.S. dollars, will be affected. The cost of Canadian goods in the United States (and of American products in Canada) depends on the exchange rate between the Canadian and U.S. dollars. If compensation measured in Canadian dollars increases somewhat to cover the extra cost of financing public health insurance benefits, the value of the Canadian dollar should fall in relation to the U.S. dollar. The cost to Americans of buying Canadian products would thus remain unaffected by the higher compensation of Canadian workers.[2]

2. Even without flexible exchange rates, real wages can adjust downward to the extent that prices increase to reflect the higher costs of the added protection or regulation.

Clearly there are some circumstances in which a generous public health insurance system can affect a country's trade patterns, as well as the location of firms and industries. For example, some industries might have very high medical costs because of unhealthy work conditions or an aged work force. Under generous public health insurance, these extra health costs are financed by the national health system rather than medical spending by the workers or their companies. This pattern of cross-subsidies can benefit some workers and firms at the expense of workers and firms in other industries. But industry, as a whole, does not suffer a cost disadvantage as a result of a national health scheme.

In any event, the fact that some industries will see their competitive positions improved by the government's provision of health insurance and others will see their positions harmed, holds whether or not a country maintains open borders. To be sure, free trade can amplify the gains and losses. In an open economy, companies whose relative costs increase by more than average as a result of better social protection face competition from overseas producers who do not bear these costs. The foreign competitors may be able to prevent the domestic companies from charging their customers the full amount of the extra costs associated with social protection or regulation. If this happens, profits and employment in the affected companies will fall. But these losses will be offset by gains enjoyed by others companies that find the added social protection reduces their costs. The bottom line is that while trade may amplify the total losses and gains, societies still face the fundamental decision of whether or not to grant the social protection: if it makes sense to offer the protection in a closed economy, it will also make sense in an open economy.

Similarly, societies that want a cleaner environment and safer workplaces should implement policies to achieve these goals, even when their economies are fully integrated with global capital and labor markets. In fact, some environmental and safety measures may improve a nation's measured productivity, by making its workers healthier and better motivated. Where this occurs, costs will fall and wages and profits may rise. In other cases, government regulation will raise costs and may reduce workers' take-home pay. But if the regulations deliver social benefits exceeding the social costs, then the regulations make sense. And they make equally good sense in open and closed economies. There are no free lunches in either kind of economy, but recognizing that a beneficial policy has costs does not mean that it should be abandoned. If the benefit-cost ratio of the policy looks acceptable in a closed economy, there is no reason to believe it will look unacceptable when the economy is opened to the free flow of trade and capital.[3]

Some liberal critics of open trade claim that the desire to attract capital induces countries to make their environmental regulations more lenient than they would actually prefer; that is, openness encourages a "race to the bottom." This argument assumes that international capital is attracted by lax regulation. This may be true for some kinds of industries with respect to some kinds of regulation. For example, firms in high-polluting industries may seek out countries with lax environmental regulation. But other companies, such as those in the tourist industry, actually prefer cleaner environments; as do many business executives who face the prospect of moving to a locality where their company has just made a big investment.[4]

The empirical evidence does not support the claim that globalization reduces environmental standards. In fact, a recent review of the literature concludes that compared to factors such as wages and transportation, differences in environmental compliance costs are a relatively minor consideration in determining production costs across countries, suggesting that environmental regulation plays a very small role in trade flows and plant location decisions.[5] Otherwise, one would have seen a mass migration of American industry out of the United States and into the high-polluting countries of the underdeveloped world.

Regulations and social safety nets do impose costs on firms. And firms that can move their operations—and jobs—across the world are

---

3. This view assumes that it is possible to exclude those who do not pay taxes from receiving benefits. If labor is internationally mobile and new immigrants are eligible for benefits, broad welfare systems (including public education and government support for health insurance) may become more difficult to operate, and the costs of the welfare system could become excessively burdensome.

4. For a theoretical discussion, see Wilson (1996).

5. Jaffe and others (1995).

relatively more likely to do so when government measures increase their labor costs. But if net wages fall to reflect the costs imposed by social regulations and the taxes needed to provide social protection, even activist governments can operate efficiently in an open economy.[6] The lesson for governments is not to restrict globalization, but to avoid policies that tax or provide public goods wastefully.

To some extent, globalization does in fact limit the ability of individual governments to redistribute income and to regulate firms' behavior. Governments that try to shift income away from activities and people that are highly mobile internationally will often fail— unless the activities or the individuals receive adequate services in return. But capital does not flee when the government raises taxes to finance infrastructure, education, and other amenities that enhance productivity. Likewise, many wealthy people, who could live anywhere, choose to live in places with high taxes, such as Manhattan or Paris, because they feel the benefits are commensurate with the costs. If high taxes were all that mattered to Bill Gates, Warren Buffett, or most of the other billionaires in America, they might have left a long time ago for other low-tax jurisdictions.[7] Despite taxes that some may claim to be too high but in reality are among the lowest in the industrialized world, the United States continues to be a magnet for people from around the world, both skilled and unskilled.

By the same token, the international mobility of direct investment— capital invested in the form of physical assets or major shareholding positions in corporations—should not be exaggerated. While portfolio investments move across the globe at lightning speed and some firms are very footloose, and thus highly sensitive to taxes and other cost-raising measures, most companies find it most advantageous to locate where they do their business. And companies that have established roots in a place face enormous costs if they move. In fact, considerable

6. Real wages can fall for any one of three reasons: if nominal wages fall; if inflation increases, eroding the real purchasing power of a given nominal wage; or if the currency depreciates, which reduces the purchasing power of a given real wage because the devaluation leads to higher import prices.

7. Nonetheless, the emerging growth of "electronic commerce," conducted over the Internet, may eventually pose a significant threat to the ability of governments to assess and collect taxes, since it is so easy for companies to move their servers and conduct business in low-tax jurisdictions; see Litan and Niskanen (1998).

evidence suggests that most investors have a very strong bias toward holding their wealth in domestic assets and most domestic saving is invested at home.[8]

One final complaint—especially in regard to advanced communication technologies and the Internet—is that precisely because it expands consumers' access to information and entertainment in addition to traditional goods and services, the emerging global culture threatens local norms as well as local providers of information and culture. Yet, as with regulation and taxation, there does not appear to be any evidence of a race to the bottom. While Hollywood and Coca-Cola are now ubiquitous, the rich array of products and artifacts available in many parts of the globe today far exceeds that available at any time in the past. Nationalists may feel that additional choice represents a reduction in human welfare, but the great majority of people clearly feels otherwise. For two centuries, residents of both rich and poor countries have gravitated to urban areas in order to take advantage of greater choice of employment and goods and services to buy. The movement *out* of big urban areas in rich societies only began when improvements in transportation and communication made it possible for people in suburban and then rural areas to enjoy a similar range of choices.

To sum up, free trade and mobile capital do not preclude a society from adopting activist social welfare policies. Globalization may complicate the ability of governments to redistribute income, either directly or through regulation. But globalization does not prevent countries from taxing foreign incomes or providing public goods through government spending, taxes, and regulation, so long as these goods (net of their tax costs) are valued by firms and people that are mobile or are paid for by those that are not.

International Trade Agreements and National Sovereignty

For an agreement, whether between two individuals or many nations, to mean anything, it must constrain the future actions of those who sign it. But just as an individual who signs a contract does not forfeit

8. Rodrik (1997).

his or her liberty, so the United States does not lose its sovereignty when it signs a trade agreement. NAFTA and the WTO, like all major trade agreements, were signed by an elected president and approved by an elected Congress. Those who objected to these agreements had the right to contest them. Many did so, and they lost the debate. Far from constraining the liberty of the citizens of the United States, this process and its results were democratic and entirely consistent with preserving national sovereignty.

The real issue raised by international trade agreements is not whether they reduce national sovereignty, but whether the specific obligations and requirements that they impose on a nation are greater or less than the benefits that nation receives from applying the same requirements to others (along with itself). According to this standard, the benefits to the United States of joining the WTO vastly outweigh the costs. By granting America most favored nation status with all 125 members, the agreement improves U.S. access to foreign markets. It also limits the ability of other nations to use protectionist measures to block U.S. access to their markets. In addition, the United States gains from WTO restrictions on its own subsidies and antidumping measures, which will reduce the domestic costs of these policies.

At the same time, WTO rules preserve the possibility of wide national differences in domestic policies. The agreement does not require nations to adopt specific policies, but does obligate them to apply policies in ways that do not discriminate against or among member nations. This principle follows article 20 of GATT:

Subject to the requirement that such measures are not applied in a manner which would constitute . . . a disguised restriction on international trade, nothing in this agreement shall be construed to prevent the adoption or enforcement by any contracting party of measures: . . . . Necessary to protect public morals, . . . human, animal or plant life or health, . . . national treasures of artistic, historic or archaeological value, the conservation of exhaustible natural resources [or] relating to the products of prison labor.[9]

9. GATT (1952).

In the final analysis, the WTO cannot compel a member nation to adhere to its provisions. If a WTO panel finds that the United States has violated any GATT rule, and the United States is unwilling to change its practices or mitigate the effect by reducing another barrier to trade, the worst that could happen is that the complaining country withdraws a trade concession that it had previously made to the United States. Critics of the WTO, such as Ralph Nader and Lori Wallach, claim that this outcome would amount to a "perpetual trade sanction."[10] But they ignore the benefits to the United States of belonging to the WTO and the costs of withdrawing from the organization. By withdrawing, the United States would lose the ability to use the WTO mechanism to induce other countries to reduce their own trade barriers, and so would hurt U.S. exporting industries and their workers.

Ultimately, no free people should yield their right to self-determination. At times, however, nations find it in their rational self-interest to subject current decisions to an external constraint, even when those decisions are determined democratically. The U.S. Constitution represents such an external constraint on the actions that voters, Congress, and the President can take today. Americans are free to amend the Constitution, but the prescribed process is intentionally quite difficult, because its authors' goal was to establish a predictable and enduring system for governing the affairs of the nation.

In much the same way, Congress has democratically chosen to enter into international trade agreements that impose constraints on national behavior. It may well be that individual nations are sometimes required to change policies that conflict with these agreements. But in doing so, they have not given up their sovereignty. On the contrary, when trade disputes arise, the offending nations can either choose to pay the

---

10. Nader and Wallach (1996). Nader and Wallach claim that "any national, state, or local standard that provides more protection than does a specified industry-shaped international standard must pass a gauntlet of WTO tests to avoid being labeled an illegal trade barrier" (p. 97). In reality, as legal scholar Alan Sykes points out, when deeply held differences of opinion arise over appropriate risk levels or scientific controversy, importing nations can find ample basis in the text of GATT to resist change in their policies. Similarly, NAFTA commits the parties to make compatible "their standards-related measures 'to the greatest extent practicable,' provided that this shall not reduce 'the level of safety or protection of human, animal or plant life or health, the environment or consumers.'" Sykes (1995, p. 108.)

penalty for violating their treaty obligations or withdraw from the agreement if its principles are no longer consistent with their interests.

Moreover, sovereignty can be shared in a variety of ways. It is rare for the principles, the regulations, and the enforcement of international agreements all to be implemented internationally. Under the WTO, general principles are adopted in international forums, but they are implemented by each nation individually, subject to a dispute settlement procedure. Under NAFTA, the issues of dumping and countervailing duties are governed by national laws, and the side agreements on labor and environmental standards are implemented nationally, but all with international oversight.

In some cases, international agreements have led to the harmonization of a variety of rules regarding economic regulation. This has occurred, for example, with respect to rules governing minimum capital requirements for banks located in the United States and some other industrialized countries. In other cases, nations have agreed to minimum standards, with each party free to adopt tougher standards. A third approach is the mutual recognition of national standards. In the European Union, for example, if a product meets the standards of any one member country, it may be sold in all of them.

Openness and Standards

International trade entails the exchange of goods from the country where they are produced to others where they are consumed. Each country can apply whatever rules it chooses, from worker safety to environmental quality, to its own part of this exchange: the producing country can regulate the production, and the consuming country can regulate the consumption.

For some critics, however, this simple principle falls short. They argue that the United States should not trade, or at a minimum, should not negotiate further reduction of trade barriers, with countries that do not live by certain basic minimum regulatory standards. For example, some opposed the Clinton administration's proposal for fast-track trade negotiating authority because it did not guarantee that the United States would negotiate only with countries that adhered to the list of labor standards developed by the International Labor Organization (ILO), including the right of workers to form unions and bargain collectively, bans on child labor and forced labor, guarantees against discrimination, and equal pay for women and men. Others criticized the fast-track proposal for falling short on environmental protections. Although they were less specific, they seemed to imply that the United States should only make agreements with countries that maintain environmental standards above a minimum threshold. Similar criticisms of liberalizing trade agreements have been raised in Europe. The European Union, for example, attempted to forbid the sale of American beef produced with hormones (but was foiled by the WTO, which ruled the attempt a violation of GATT).[11]

To evaluate these claims, it is vital to distinguish between two regulatory settings. On the one hand, certain regulations and activities in one country can directly affect other countries. As discussed in chapter 5, pollution that crosses national borders offers a clear illustration of such an externality. Similarly, one country's immigration rules may affect the size of the labor force in another country. In these cases, there is a good argument for international rules or coordination.[12] The United States has recognized as much by participating in such international forums as the Rio Conference on the world environment and the International Labor Organization.

On the other hand are those regulations aimed at activities that are purely local in nature. Most labor standards and human rights policies fall into this category. The rules established by Singapore or Thailand for their employers and workers—with respect to minimum wages, child labor, and the right to belong to a union, for example—directly affect employers and workers only in those countries. Any effects that

---

11. Nonetheless, WTO rules provide countries with considerable leeway, especially with respect to public health, to protect their citizens from any harmful impact of imports. In the case of the dispute over beef hormones, even though the European Union's objections were overruled, it could still have refused to import American beef. But if it did so, the United States would be entitled to seek compensation under WTO procedures.

12. If countries aim to share a single labor market (that is, if they allow workers to migrate without restriction, as the European Union has attempted to do), there is a stronger case for participating nations to agree to common labor standards than when immigration is subject to controls.

these rules might have on other countries are indirect and occur only through normal investment and trade flows. In this case it is reasonable to ask whether it is appropriate for any country to impose its values on others. Citizens of the United States may agree, for example, that forcing a country to allow its workers to organize will produce a more equitable distribution of income, or that workplace safety regulation will increase people's willingness to work. But even assuming that applying such standards will produce benefits, the question remains why one country should be able to force another to take such steps.

The world is very diverse, and one nation's sacred cow may be the next country's favorite meal. There is no assurance that imposing the same standards on countries where conditions and norms differ will produce optimal, or even desirable, results. For example, tough environmental standards will likely reduce pollution, but usually at significant cost, which countries with lenient standards may simply be unable to bear. As a rule, if one is offended by a country's behavior in some area, one should be prepared to shoulder the costs of changing it, as does the European Union in providing substantial transfers to its poorer members while insisting that those members adopt higher, community standards.

In the debates over fast-track authority, representatives of labor organizations have argued that tying the negotiation of trade issues to labor standards is no different than seeking to have other countries strengthen their rules of intellectual property. In both cases, they allege, the United States is seeking to impose its views and values on other countries. This analogy is misplaced. Labor standards may affect trade, but they do not constitute a trade barrier.[13] By contrast, weak intellectual property rules can act as barriers to trade: U.S. software companies will be strongly discouraged from exporting their programs to countries where they can be easily copied without penalty. These critics would also do well to remember that by crusading to have the rest of the world adopt standards similar to its own, the United States opens itself to crusading by others, who could charge, for example, that its treatment of migrant workers or its weak effort to reduce

---

13. Indeed, the empirical evidence suggests that even weak labor standards do not have a statistically significant effect on trade flows; Golub (1997).

energy consumption constitute "unfair" practices that artificially distort trade in its favor.

More broadly, there is some irony in the claim that it is in America's self-interest to insist that other nations meet tough environmental and labor standards. Any harms alleged to flow from lax standards are suffered by *foreign residents,* not those of the United States. To the extent that a nation's principal environmental goal is to protect its own air and water, a policy of openness actually improves the local environment. If its trade policy were guided only by economic self-interest, the United States should be eager to import goods produced in countries with weak labor and environmental standards. It could then specialize in producing goods and services that do not generate pollution and that economize on unskilled labor. Air and water would be cleaner in America and the evil side effects of pollution and weak labor standards would be borne by people abroad.[14] Therefore it is somewhat odd to argue that the United States should sacrifice bargaining chips in trade negotiations to fight for benefits that will accrue mainly to foreigners. Should it not instead fight for benefits that mainly benefit Americans and let foreigners worry about the welfare of their own citizens? We do not argue that the quality of the environment in foreign countries should be of no concern to Americans. We think it is foolish to treat this concern as a matter of our economic self-interest, however.

Many environmentalists do want to improve the environment overseas as well as at home. However, they must face up to the fact that there is a limit to America's ability to affect environmental policies abroad. Foreign policymakers who do not share environmentalists' views will only be induced to accept minimum environmental standards if other countries offer significant aid or trade concessions in return. To the extent that U.S. policymakers grant these, they will be using up some of their bargaining power in persuading foreign governments to open up local markets to U.S. and other producers. One must therefore be prepared to give up some degree of access to other markets in order to gain "concessions" on environmental (or labor) standards for the benefit of citizens of other countries.

14. As discussed above, this proposition does not hold when pollution crosses national boundaries. But much pollution reduces the quality of life only for local residents, not people living thousands of miles away.

Advocates of "standards linkage" must also honestly confront the reality that insisting that another country adopt tougher labor and environmental standards for its citizens will reduce the likelihood that any agreement is reached. In this light, it is legitimate to ask whether the real purpose of those who favor standards linkage in trade deals is to help those overseas or protect certain workers at home.

For example, to prevent "unfair" competition in coal mining in other countries, one might insist that any trade agreement contain tough health and safety standards that force foreign companies to produce coal with the same risk to coal miners as that faced by their counterparts in the United States. Yet for countries lacking the technologies or safety equipment available in the United States, this may be practically impossible—as indeed it would have been in the United States thirty or forty years ago. Even though the rhetoric behind the American bargaining position may stress the importance of improving mining safety standards abroad, in reality the effect of having other countries adopt this position is to protect coal mining in the United States.

Or consider those who advocate that other countries adopt strict labor standards, professing the laudable intent of improving the welfare of foreign workers. Is this the best way to help these workers? Or is it better to offer their countries liberalized trade, which expands employment opportunities in export industries abroad? Even though jobs in these industries offer wages and working conditions that may be appalling by U.S. standards, they are often the best jobs available to unskilled workers in the developing world. Is it humane for the United States to refuse to trade with these countries because their labor standards are not as high as we would prefer? The consequence of taking this position is that many third-world workers will have no jobs at all, or must take jobs that pay even lower wages and have even worse working conditions than those currently available in the export-oriented sector.

Paul Krugman sums up the matter in this way:

> Are those who want to impose import restrictions against countries with low labor standards willing to lift those restrictions against countries that start to pay decent wages? Circa 1970 Japan was still a low-wage country, accused of keeping its workers in "rabbit hutches" in order to pursue its relentless export drive. By the early 1990s Japanese wages were

actually higher than those in the United States. Did the Japan-bashers relent? In 1975 South Korean wages were only 5 percent of those in the United States; by 1995 they had risen to 43 percent. Did opposition to Korean exports dissipate? The real complaint against developing countries is not that their exports are based on low wages and sweatshops. The complaint is that they export at all.[15]

But suppose that Krugman is wrong and that those who press linkage between standards and trade genuinely want to assist workers abroad. Putting aside whether linkage will actually achieve that objective, voters and policymakers must ask what price, in terms of lost opportunities to gain access to foreign markets, Americans are willing to pay to help others abroad. Not much, we suspect, judging from the unpopularity of government-financed foreign aid programs. Those who argue vigorously for standards linkage rarely, if ever, explain that they are effectively advocating a type of foreign aid program that is financed by selectively higher prices on certain imports and lost job opportunities in American export industries. Those industries might gain additional sales if the United States could obtain reduced trade barriers from its foreign trade partners, concessions it is less likely to achieve if it insists on high labor standards.

It is possible that a country's behavior may be so reprehensible—through the practice of apartheid or slavery, or the massacre or abuse of innocent civilians—that another nation may unilaterally refuse to trade with it. But these cases are rare. When a country chooses such a course, it must be prepared to accept that it may impose real costs on its own producers and consumers, and occasionally on the victims overseas whom it is trying to help.

When there is no national consensus, individual consumers are of course free to apply their own private sanctions. Anyone who believes that child labor or forced labor are wrong can choose not to buy products from countries that allow these practices. International bodies, such as the ILO, could facilitate consumer pressure by publishing lists of "offending" countries, as well as of those countries that inhibit ILO inspectors from ascertaining whether such practices are current, much

15. Krugman (1997a).

as various human rights organizations already do. If a majority of voters believes that sufficient and accurate information is not being made available for consumers to make their purchasing decisions, national governments can disseminate such information to their own citizens. The U.S. government can help American consumers in this way by requiring sellers in its market to accurately label their products with the country of origin, and encouraging them to identify those that are "environmentally safe" or "dolphin friendly."[16]

Conclusion

The claim that globalization has cost the United States its sovereignty is intellectually bankrupt. The United States enters into trade deals to advance its economic interests. To be sure, the global economy puts some constraints on both private and public sector decisionmaking, but the costs of these constraints pale in comparison with the economic benefits that Americans derive from freer trade. If the United States were less closely integrated with the rest of the world on economic matters, its citizens, as a group, would be worse off.

Globalization does not confer equal benefits on everyone, and indeed, some workers may be made worse off as a result of freer international flows of goods and capital. The challenge for policymakers is to find effective ways to cushion the blow suffered by those workers. For at least two reasons this kind of policy makes sense. It is the equitable and humane thing to do. As a practical matter, moreover, if the legitimate concerns of those who lose out or are threatened by free trade are not addressed, policymakers will face increasing political pressure to reverse the trade liberalization that so far has brought significant benefits to the U.S. economy.

---

16. Admittedly, labeling does not eliminate the harm caused by objectionable practices. When fully informed consumers refuse to buy products made by slave labor, they avoid the psychological damage that they might suffer if they unwittingly purchased products of slave labor. But unless millions of other consumers join them in their boycott, the real evil of slavery is likely to persist.

7 ADDRESSING DISLOCATION AND INEQUALITY

n the preceding chapters we have tried to make one thing clear: few of the globaphobic attacks on closer world economic integration have any merit. America's growing economic links with the rest of the world are not responsible for slower average income growth, higher unemployment, or the productivity slowdown. Closer economic integration accounts for at most a small fraction of the job loss in manufacturing and the increased disparity in U.S. wages.[1] The charge that American workers and companies must compete on an unlevel international playing field reflects a fundamental misunderstanding of what trade and exchange are all about. The point of trade is to exploit the advantages of differences between nations. The gains from trade would be vastly smaller if all countries were identical.

Globalization has not undermined U.S. sovereignty. Pleas that the United States should negotiate trade agreements only with countries that meet minimum environmental and labor standards ignore the interests of U.S. consumers and exporters. Even if negotiators heeded these pleas, they would not necessarily improve the welfare of low-income workers in the third world, the supposed beneficiaries of minimum labor standards. In many cases, U.S. insistence on minimum standards would choke the expansion of the modern sector in third

---

1. Recent immigration trends have probably played a larger role in the growing inequality of wages, as discussed in chapter 4.

world countries, limiting poor workers' chances of improving their living standards.

If the intellectual case for globaphobia is weak, why does global competition continue to arouse so much fear among ordinary Americans? Why is globaphobia so attractive in the political marketplace? We believe the fundamental reason is that fear of global integration taps into a large reservoir of public anxiety about slow income growth, potential job loss, rising inequality, and a seeming loss of control of our economic destiny. Notwithstanding a twenty-five-year low in the national unemployment rate, many Americans remain fearful that, with little notice, they could be the victims of "downsizing" or be "reengineered" out of a job.

In spite of this fear, voters appear unwilling to pay higher taxes to cover major increases in government spending on assistance or tax relief for lower income workers, even though such spending might reduce workers' income insecurity and offset part of the effect of wider pay disparities. Voters' reluctance to fund such initiatives is not hard to explain. Slower economic growth has made Americans less willing to be taxed, and voters' experience with previous public initiatives has given them little confidence that a major expansion in government would in fact reduce their insecurity.

Throwing sand in the gears of globalization, by contrast, represents tangible action that politicians can take to change the situation. Even better, it requires no additional government spending. While economists may poke holes in protectionist theories and evidence, critics of global integration can point to apparently persuasive anecdotes and facts: anemic wage growth, identifiable workers thrown out of jobs, plants relocated to offshore sites, and claims by management that these unhappy steps are all necessary because of the evil effects of global competition. Elevating U.S. barriers to foreign trade, or refusing to enter new trade deals with low-wage countries, if nothing else, offers the comforting illusion that these developments can be reversed or halted.

Those who believe, as we do, that closer economic integration is in America's best interest must address the legitimate concerns that underlie the nation's fear of integration. When open trade policies that benefit the country as a whole also exact a price from certain groups of workers, the country has a responsibility in some way to make amends. In addition, failing to do so would court a growing voter backlash that could reverse the progress already made toward more open markets and unravel the economic gains that the United States has enjoyed as a result of this progress. The danger is already plain. Fueled by deep public skepticism, many members of Congress bitterly attacked American participation in the financial rescue that helped to prevent Mexico from defaulting on its foreign debt in 1995. Congress now routinely rejects pleas for additional U.S. capital contributions to the World Bank and International Monetary Fund, even though these institutions play a crucial role in maintaining the stability of the world financial system, in which the United States is an important participant and beneficiary. In late 1997 Congress refused to grant the President what would once have been routine authorization to negotiate trade deals on a fast-track basis. This inaction limits the administration's ability to make deals that will open new foreign markets to U.S. exports in exchange for greater openness of the U.S. market. In the next recession, there could be significantly greater risk that the United States will take aggressive steps to close its markets to foreigners, reversing the direction of America's post-war trade policy.

We offer no silver bullets to resolve the economic problems that give rise to globaphobia. In 1993 two authors of this book (Burtless and Litan) outlined a set of proposals designed to yield major improvements in both economic growth and the equitable distribution of the benefits of prosperity.[2] Their proposals included a number of initiatives: a major reduction in the federal budget deficit, which, by lowering interest rates would help to spur an increase in private investment; doubling the federal tax credit for private research and development; restoring generous tax treatment of companies' spending on plant and equipment; measures to increase the level and improve the equity of public and private spending on worker training; and initiatives to liberalize the rules governing foreign trade and investment, as well as a new strategy to encourage U.S. trade partners to liberalize their own rules. The first of these proposals was adopted and is now reflected in U.S. budget policy. In response, American private investment jumped

2. Baily, Burtless, and Litan (1993).

significantly, as we expected, both absolutely and as a share of total U.S. output. A couple of other proposals, including improvement in the research and development tax credit, have also been implemented in some form. Productivity growth has picked up somewhat since 1993, but income inequality has fallen only slightly.

Another author of this book (Shapiro) previously has proposed spurring long-term growth through a major shift in the tax and spending policies of the federal government: by phasing out industry-specific tax and spending subsidies, reducing the federal workforce and administrative costs, and shifting the resources to deficit reduction and targeted public investments in education, infrastructure and research and development. He also has offered proposals for reforming the tax system and the public provision of education and job training. Some of these proposals have been adopted, others not.

Other critics of U.S. economic performance have made more ambitious proposals to boost the nation's growth rate. From the right come calls for a large cut in the capital gains tax rate (to which the administration acceded), or an ambitious shift toward a flat-rate income or consumption tax. Both kinds of reform, it is alleged, will help to unleash a wave of investment and entrepreneurial activity, leading to faster overall growth. Not only are we skeptical of these claims, we think that tax reform along these lines would worsen the country's other main economic problem: increased inequality.

At the other end of the political spectrum, liberals have advanced proposals to boost public spending on education, transportation, and other public activities that might help the economy to grow faster. Yet spending more money without fundamentally reforming the way money is used will probably have only a small impact on the "outputs" of these public activities. Fundamental reform involves improving the incentives for efficient and effective delivery of these public services. This might be achieved, for example, by increasing students' incentives to learn or raising charges on highway users during periods of peak use. An even more basic problem with the liberal approach is that in an era of balanced budgets, it seems unlikely that there will be substantial additional public funds for a growth agenda. More public resources will only become available if political leaders can persuade

Americans to accept higher taxes, a prospect that in 1998 seems highly unlikely.

Neither party's leaders seem willing to take big steps to address the problem of growing inequality. To be sure, this issue has generated a new wave of interest in academia. Edmund Phelps of Columbia University has proposed that the federal government launch a massive program to subsidize the wages of workers stuck at the bottom of the pay scale.[3] This would effectively boost the take-home pay of a subsidized worker toward $8 an hour, while leaving employers' wage costs unchanged or even reduced. The subsidy would spur employment growth and at the same time reduce the inequality of take-home pay. Bruce Ackerman and Anne Alstot of the Yale Law School propose an even more audacious plan to provide equal opportunity.[4] They would offer all young adults a minimum cash "stake" in American society equal to $80,000. New labor market entrants could invest their stakes in further education, specialized training, establishing a new business, or any one of a wide range of other activities. This plan would certainly level the playing field of initial opportunity in America, though at enormous public expense over the next several decades. In the current political environment, neither the Phelps nor the Ackerman-Alstot proposal is politically feasible. But this type of scholarly attention may lay the intellectual groundwork for the eventual development of politically palatable solutions.

Our ambitions in this book are narrower. The persistent problems of slow growth and rising inequality are both serious public issues, and any solutions are beyond the scope of this volume. Instead, in this concluding chapter we offer suggestions for addressing the economic dislocations suffered by workers and firms as a result of liberalized trade. Economists have long recognized that while free trade confers net benefits on the economy as a whole, it also inflicts harm on certain workers and firms, who suffer economic losses as a result of the increased competition created by liberalized trade. A standard remedy for the economic fallout from free trade is to require that the winners share some of their gains with the losers through some form of compensa-

3. Phelps (1997).
4. Ackerman and Alstot (1998).

tion. We take this seriously as a political requirement and a moral obligation.

Addressing Dislocation from All Sources

It is useful to begin by briefly reviewing current government policies that shelter workers from economic losses whatever the cause, trade related or not. Trade is just one of many sources of change in a dynamic economy. The economist Joseph Schumpeter observed that healthy capitalism produces an environment of "creative destruction." Capitalist markets operate by displacing old ideas, products, and methods of production with new and better ones. The great majority of consumers and producers eventually benefits from this process, and the overwhelming majority adapts to it in some fashion. But a few workers and producers suffer sizable and permanent losses along the way.

Governments have established a variety of safety net programs to help workers cope with the insecurity that is inevitable in an environment of creative destruction. These programs not only protect individuals from the worst side effects of change, they also help to reduce the income disparities that occur even in a smoothly functioning economy. We think that the American safety net programs can be improved to reduce the insecurity that workers face in the new global economy. At the same time, some of our proposed changes can moderate the wide disparities in U.S. incomes.

From the point of view of working men and women, one of the most important components of the safety net is unemployment insurance. The U.S. unemployment insurance system was established as part of the Social Security Act legislated during the Great Depression. The program assumed its present form and scale shortly after World War II. The system serves two crucial functions. It provides workers with essential income protection when they are temporarily unemployed as a result of a layoff. And by helping unemployed workers maintain consumption in bad times, it also gives the economy a welcome stimulus when overall unemployment is high.

Each of the fifty states maintains its own unemployment program, which collectively cover more than 97 percent of wage and salary workers. All of the state programs have several important features in common. Workers gain eligibility for unemployment benefits by working a minimum period of time in jobs that are covered by the system. When workers are laid off, they file claims for weekly benefits that can last up to about six months or until they are reemployed, whichever occurs sooner. For workers who earn average or below average wages, the weekly benefit replaces about half of lost wages. Because states impose a cap on weekly benefits, highly paid workers do not receive such a high percentage of their lost earnings. The average unemployment check in 1996 was about $190 a week. States with particularly high rates of unemployment offer extended benefits that may add as much as three months to the six months of benefits that are ordinarily available. When the national unemployment rate is high, Congress sometimes authorizes further extensions of benefits that can add two to four additional months to the period of eligibility. In general, workers who are unemployed longer than six months may apply for food stamps or public assistance benefits, but eligibility for these benefits is limited by strict income and asset tests.

Although most Americans agree that unemployment insurance is an essential part of the safety net, many would also acknowledge that the program creates some serious incentive problems for unemployed workers. Because the unemployment check replaces a large percentage of the earnings lost as a result of unemployment, it reduces pressure on the worker to accept another job. This can be a good thing if it gives workers the luxury of rejecting bad job offers and continuing to look for better prospects. But the weekly check creates adverse incentives when it allows workers to postpone a serious search for a new job or encourages them to reject good job offers. In both these cases, taxpayers are obliged to continue paying for unemployment benefits to the worker, even though the worker is not productively or seriously engaged in finding a job. The unemployment insurance system ends up subsidizing a vacation for the unemployed worker, rather than encouraging the worker to find a job quickly or track down the best possible job lead. In our discussion of compensation programs for trade-affected workers, we suggest a major extension of unemployment insurance that would significantly reduce the adverse incentives of the program.

Government education and training programs offer a second line of defense to some workers who have been thrown out of a job. Unemployed workers who enroll in these programs can improve their job qualifications, making it easier for them to find new jobs—possibly better jobs than the ones they lost. The federal government has established a number of programs to finance worker training, although most of the funds are earmarked for low-income workers or workers in targeted groups, including the welfare population. In comparison with the tens of millions of workers who lose their jobs each year, these programs are quite modest in size. Spending by the U.S. Department of Labor on training programs amounted to just $5.2 billion in 1997, or roughly one-fifth of the funds spent on unemployment insurance. About $1.3 billion of the training funds was devoted to providing assistance to experienced workers who lost their jobs as a result of plant closings or mass layoffs. The purpose of this spending is to help states and local communities give job search help, training, and relocation assistance to displaced workers. But only about half a million workers participated in the dislocated worker program in 1997.

Government help is not limited to worker retraining programs, however. State and local governments provide substantial assistance to students attending public two- and four-year colleges. This is provided directly, through scholarships, and indirectly, through operational subsidies to public colleges. In addition, the federal government offers subsidized student loans to college students as well as to participants in proprietary training programs, and it gives educational and training grants to students from low-income families. Congress appropriated almost $12 billion for federal student loans and grants in 1997. Although these funds are available to people who lose jobs as a result of economic change, most of the money is used by recent high school graduates and young adults who have not yet begun their careers. Most older workers correctly believe they have already accumulated enough skill and job experience to support themselves in the job market. When they lose their jobs they may need some retraining, but most workers over the age of thirty are reluctant to begin a multiyear course of college study. To most unemployed adult workers, government subsidies for retraining or college education do not seem particularly attractive.

Another component of the safety net that is relevant to low-income workers is the Earned Income Tax Credit (EITC). The credit is a refundable tax rebate paid directly to families with low earnings. It provides up to $3,556 a year to low-income workers who support two or more children, and smaller amounts to childless workers and those who support one child. The tax credit is essentially an earnings supplement to top up the wages of family breadwinners who earn low pay. It is not available to low-income families unless at least one member does earn wages, and it grows as the breadwinner's earnings rise, up to a limit. For a breadwinner with one child, the credit rises $0.34 for every $1.00 in additional wages, up to an annual wage limit of $6,330. For breadwinners with two or more children, the credit rises $0.40 for every $1.00 in additional earnings up to an annual limit of $8,890. The maximum credit is therefore $2,152 for a one-child family and $3,556 for a family with two or more children. The credit is gradually phased out once the breadwinner's annual earnings rise above $11,610.[5]

Unlike most government aid programs for low-income families, the EITC creates a substantial work incentive, at least for potential breadwinners who do not initially work or who work only a few hours. Workers who lose well-paying jobs and are forced to accept poorly paid jobs can receive major benefits under the credit. For example, a single worker who is laid off from a job paying $25,000 a year and forced to accept a job at $13,000 receives a credit of about $1,900 if the worker has one child, or $3,300 with two or more children. This credit continues as long as the worker's wages remain stuck at $13,000. The credit thus offsets part of the earnings loss that the worker must accept when taking a new job.

The social safety net for working-age families would be much stronger if it assured workers and their dependents of health insurance benefits. In contrast with the governments of other industrialized coun-

5. These dollar amounts were in effect in 1996. The earnings limits and phase-out amounts are adjusted each year, in line with inflation.

tries, the U.S. government does not provide, or require employers to provide, health insurance to workers or their dependents. In 1996, nearly 42 million Americans—more than one in seven—were not covered by a public or private health insurance plan during any part of the year.[6] While most of the uninsured were workers and dependents of workers, many of the unemployed also lacked insurance—many had lost their health coverage with their last jobs. Most uninsured Americans have some access to low-cost or free emergency medical care through public hospitals, charity care in private hospitals, or public health clinics. Nonetheless, lack of health insurance coverage limits people's choice of doctors and hospitals and discourages them from receiving beneficial care. Many workers recognize that when they lose their jobs they may eventually lose access to affordable health insurance, even if they find another job. We suspect that much of Americans' anxiety about job loss stems from their fear that they may lose essential health coverage permanently.

The Clinton administration failed in its attempt to secure a national system offering universal and comprehensive health insurance coverage. We do not pretend to know what alternative plan would have won broader popular support. Voters may approve of the idea of universal insurance coverage, but few who already enjoy good coverage can be persuaded to pay higher premiums or taxes to assure that the rest of the population also has access to good insurance. Both federal and state lawmakers have found voters are more willing to pay for higher public spending that is devoted to improving health coverage for children. Public money has been spent to extend children's coverage in several ways. With federal prodding and generous subsidies, state governments have been encouraged to offer free health insurance under medicaid to a larger percentage of children in low-income families. On their own initiative, states have established subsidized health insurance programs for low-income workers and their child dependents. In 1997 Congress offered additional federal subsidies to encourage all states to offer subsidized plans for low-income children who are not covered by medicaid.

6. Bennefield (1997, p. 1).

While these steps will increase the percentage of children that is covered by insurance, they will not ease most workers' anxiety about the possibility of losing health coverage when they lose a job. A useful expansion of the unemployment insurance program would provide public subsidies to the unemployed, so that they could continue to pay for insurance coverage for the first eighteen months after they lose their jobs. A 1985 federal law already requires that employers who do provide health insurance offer laid-off workers a continuation of health coverage for at least eighteen months after the date of termination. The law gives these former workers the right to maintain, at their own expense, coverage under the health plan at a cost comparable to what it would be if the laid-off workers were still members of the employer's group. However, because few employers continue to subsidize the cost of the worker's participation after layoff, the premium is effectively higher and many jobless workers cannot afford continued coverage.

A partial remedy for this problem is to subsidize laid-off workers' premium payments out of the federal unemployment insurance trust fund.[7] For example, workers with annual family incomes below $75,000 might qualify for these subsidies for up to eighteen months, so long as they remained unemployed or were not covered by another employer's health plan. The cost of this improvement in unemployment protection could be covered by a change in the federal unemployment insurance tax. Employers now pay unemployment taxes only on the money wages that they pay to workers. To finance subsidies for continued health coverage, employers who offer health insurance could be taxed on their contributions to their employee health plan. Employers that do not offer health insurance would not pay any additional tax, but their laid-off employees would not be entitled to subsidies for health insurance in the event of layoff. While this plan offers no relief to those not covered by employer health plans, it provides an extra measure of security to the 84 percent of full-time and 78 percent of part-time workers who are insured under an employer-sponsored plan.[8]

7. Robert Shapiro abstains from the discussion and policy recommendations advanced from this point in the chapter to its conclusion.
8. Bennefield (1997, p. 2).

Addressing Trade-Induced Dislocation

While basic safety net programs are crucial to the protection of all workers who suffer dislocation, there is a pragmatic reason why it is necessary to have additional targeted assistance, tied to trade-induced disruptions. In contrast to the changes in aggregate demand, technology, and management practice that may cause some workers to lose their jobs, dislocations caused by trade are often much more visible, and thus attractive, targets for political intervention. Indeed, trade is singled out in the U.S. Constitution. While the Constitution prohibits interference with interstate commerce, it expressly grants Congress the authority to regulate international commerce. Federal lawmakers are thus exposed to intense political pressure from groups that may lose from changes in the nation's trade laws. For purely political reasons, it is thus appropriate to provide temporary aid to workers and firms adversely affected by trade developments. When such aid accompanies new trade agreements, it can reduce the political opposition to freer trade. We recognize, though, that not even the most generous compensation program is likely to completely eliminate such opposition.

U.S. law already contains two provisions to cushion the adverse impacts of trade. At best, these have been only moderately effective in helping companies and workers hurt by trade and dampening the opposition to free trade. Both could use major improvement.

The Escape Clause

Current U.S. law aids firms (and their workers) that are hurt by trade by allowing the President, on the affirmative recommendation of the International Trade Commission, to authorize temporary protection against imports that are found to cause "serious injury" to a domestic industry. Embodied as section 201 of the Trade Act of 1974 (as amended) and permitted under article 19 of the General Agreement on Tariffs and Trade (GATT), it is called an escape clause because it operates as a safety valve, reducing political pressure for even more far-reaching protection. Indeed, the 1974 changes in section 201 helped to dissuade Congress from enacting an across-the-board increase in U.S. tariffs.[9]

Import relief under section 201 and GATT's article 19 has several distinctive features. First, the relief is explicitly temporary. As a result of the 1994 Uruguay Round agreement, section 201 was modified to limit import protection for an industry initially to just four years, with possible extension to a maximum of eight years. Second, the President's decision to grant import relief under section 201 is discretionary. Section 201 relief thus differs from antidumping and countervailing duties, which automatically come into force once the amount of dumping or subsidization has been quantified and found to have caused "material injury." Third, article 19 requires that countries impose escape clause protection in a nondiscriminatory way. This means that any tariffs or quotas imposed must apply to imports from all countries, not just to one or a handful of countries that may have been the focus of a domestic industry's complaints. Finally, article 19 also requires nations that use the escape clause to provide compensation to countries whose exports would be adversely affected (although if the protection lasts for fewer than three years, exporters are not permitted to suspend concessions of equivalent value, which reduces their leverage in demanding compensation).

These limitations on escape clause relief have the salutary effect of minimizing the damage that temporary protection inflicts on consumers. For that reason, however, the limitations provide import-competing industries with strong incentives to find other, more certain and permanent, methods of obtaining protection. One favored alternative is misleadingly called a voluntary restraint agreement (VRA). Under such an agreement, an importing country effectively imposes specific export constraints on a trading partner through a "voluntary" mutual agreement. The United States has entered into a variety of VRAs over the years. These have covered other countries' exports of a wide range of products, including apparel and textiles, automobiles, books, dairy products, meat, peanuts, sugar, and steel. As "voluntary" agreements, they allow countries to circumvent the nondiscrimination and com-

9. Lawrence and Litan (1986, p. 25).

pensation requirements of article 19. At least in the case of agreements negotiated by the United States, VRAs have provided more lasting protection than has section 201.[10] To thwart the use of VRAs, the Uruguay Round agreement limits each country to only one such agreement until 1999, after which they are prohibited.

Whether the Uruguay Round amendments prove successful in channeling complaints about imports into the temporary provisions of section 201 depends in large part on the extent to which domestic industries make use of the antidumping and countervailing duty remedies permitted under both U.S. law and GATT. As noted, relief under these provisions is automatic and is available under a standard ("material injury") that is easier to meet than that required under section 201 ("serious injury"). Moreover, as discussed in chapter 5, antidumping laws punish pricing behavior by foreign sellers that is lawful for their domestic competitors. This no doubt explains the growing popularity among other countries of adopting U.S.-style antidumping measures.

A key objective of future trade negotiations should be for the United States to offer the reform—even elimination—of its perverse antidumping laws to those countries that maintain adequate competition policies; that is, policies that ensure their domestic markets are not artificially distorted by private restraints of trade, which can be just as damaging to foreign competitors as the formal barriers imposed by governments.[11] In exchange, those countries would agree to eliminate or reform their antidumping laws in the same fashion. Obvious initial candidates for such a "grand bargain" include the members of the European Community, which has established a tradition of active antitrust enforcement. Once such an agreement were reached, it could provide a powerful incentive for other countries to upgrade their competition policies and enforcement activities. For its part, the United

10. Lawrence and Litan (1986, p. 49).

11. One useful reform of the current antidumping provisions would be to change the rules governing pricing "below cost," as applied to those countries deemed to have adequate competition policies in place. The new rules should conform to standards for determining "predatory pricing" under U.S. antitrust law; predatory price standards use variable rather than average costs as the benchmark for determining prohibited behavior. Another improvement to antidumping law would be to rule out the possibility of a finding of dumping simply as a result of exchange rate movements.

States would improve the fairness of its own laws while gaining for U.S. exporters improved access to foreign markets. Furthermore, by reducing the attractiveness and accessibility of antidumping remedies, arrangements of this type would also close off the route most attractive to domestic firms for bypassing the temporary import protection provisions of section 201.[12]

Trade Adjustment Assistance

A second mechanism for easing the pain of trade-induced dislocation under current U.S. law is Trade Adjustment Assistance (TAA). This program offers cash benefits and retraining to workers who lose their jobs as a result of trade. It provides extended unemployment insurance payments—Trade Readjustment Allowances (TRAs)—after the six-month limit on regular insurance payments, and also provides job search assistance, worker retraining, and relocation expenses. TAA was established in 1962 and most recently revised as part of the 1988 Trade Act. The 1988 reform for the first time made the weekly cash benefits conditional on eligible workers being enrolled in a training program or completing training. Since 1974, about 2 million workers have been certified as eligible for TAA benefits (see table 7-1). Not all of these workers actually received assistance, however, because many of them found jobs before they became entitled to collect benefits under the program.

While we approve of the goals of the current TAA program, we believe that its design is seriously flawed. The program provides little tangible compensation to workers adversely affected by trade. It offers cash aid in a way that slows down rather than accelerates adjustment to trade-induced dislocation. And it provides noncash assistance in a form that is not particularly attractive or useful to most adult workers. Not surprisingly, the program has had little effect in reducing workers' fierce opposition to freer trade.

12. The Uruguay Round agreement required antidumping and countervailing duty orders that had been on the books for at least five years to be "sunset," or reviewed, starting in late 1998. In theory, this should make many of the orders temporary, bringing them in line with similar requirements limiting import protection under the escape clause. However, it remains to be seen how many U.S. antidumping orders actually will be sunset under the review process.

TABLE 7-1. Workers Certified Eligible for Trade Adjusted Assistance since 1974, by Industry

Industry	Number
Automotive equipment	803,000
Apparel	457,000
Primary metals	218,000
Electrical equipment	206,000
Oil and gas	161,000
Leather	134,000
Fabricated metal products	62,000

Source: USTR (1996).

One major structural flaw in TAA is in its provision of cash payments. The program offers weekly cash allowances that are an extension of regular unemployment insurance benefits. The weekly benefits have the same value as regular unemployment compensation, are payable when a worker exhausts the regular benefits, and can last up to a year. Thus together, regular unemployment insurance and TRA cash benefits may stretch to eighteen months. As already noted, workers receiving unemployment compensation have an incentive to delay finding a job, sometimes until their eligibility for benefits is exhausted. The longer they delay finding a job, the more unemployment checks and TRA allowances they receive. Many analysts who have studied the impact of a lengthy unemployment spell on a worker's chances of reemployment conclude that employers tend to discount the qualifications of a job applicant more the longer the applicant has been unemployed. By providing additional weeks of benefit eligibility, TAA adds to the adverse incentives already present in unemployment insurance. Thus the cash payments slow down rather than speed up worker adjustment.

A second flaw lies in the 1988 reform that required workers eligible for TRA cash allowances to be enrolled in a training program or to have completed training. The goal of this modification seemed sensible: by requiring new skills in exchange for the cash benefits, Congress encouraged trade-displaced workers to obtain training. In theory, the training could reduce the wage losses that such workers often suffer when they are reemployed. In practice, economists find little evidence that government-sponsored training has pared the wage losses of trade-displaced workers. In the most comprehensive study of the issue, Paul Decker and Walter Corson conclude that TAA-financed training fails to produce a positive impact on earnings, at least during the first three years after displacement occurs.[13] These findings suggest that the skepticism that many displaced workers feel about the benefits of additional education or classroom training is well founded. In view of this fact, the value of the formal training promised by TAA must seem slight to a worker displaced by trade or facing imminent job displacement.[14]

A third major flaw of the TAA program is that it fails to compensate trade-displaced workers for the most important component of their economic loss: the drop in earnings that many suffer when they take a new job. Economists have found that when experienced workers are displaced from long-tenure jobs, their eventual earnings losses can amount to as much as 25 percent of their previous pay. Younger workers, workers with shorter job tenure, and workers in low-wage industries (such as footwear and apparel) do not face wage losses this large, mainly because their predisplacement wages do not have as far to fall. For displaced workers who were earning average or above-average pay, however, most of these losses typically result from earning smaller weekly paychecks, rather than from experiencing unemployment immediately after displacement.[15]

The serious flaws in TAA can be remedied by converting the program into a system of time-limited earnings insurance.[16] Earnings insurance would provide monthly or quarterly earnings supplements to compensate trade-displaced workers for a percentage of the wage losses they suffer as a result of displacement. If the program insured

13. Decker and Corson (1995). An earlier and broader review of the evidence on training for displaced workers reached the same conclusion; see Leigh (1991).

14. TAA also pays for special job search assistance to workers displaced by trade. There is stronger evidence that this kind of help can be of tangible benefit to laid-off workers with extensive job experience. Well-designed job search programs can speed up reemployment, especially among workers who have not tried to find a job very recently. Leigh (1989.)

15. See Jacobson, LaLonde, and Sullivan (1992, 1993).

16. We have advocated wage insurance plans elsewhere, albeit with somewhat different features than the plan outlined here; see Lawrence and Litan (1986) and Baily, Burtless, and Litan (1993).

workers for 50 percent of their earnings loss, for example, a displaced worker whose previous wage was $2,000 a month and was forced to accept a new job that paid only $1,000 a month would receive a monthly check of $500. The replacement or compensation ratio could be the same for all eligible workers, or it could vary with a worker's age or previous job tenure. We see a good case, on equity grounds, for providing better insurance to older workers. These workers often find it harder than younger workers to land a new job. They are also more likely to be forced to accept a large and permanent cut in their hourly wage. However, insurance should only be available to workers who have a minimum job tenure (say, two years) with their last employer. We see little economic or equity justification for providing compensatory payments to employees who suffer displacement after working only briefly with an employer.

The total amount of compensation provided to a worker in any year should be capped, say, at $10,000. This would prevent highly compensated workers from receiving extraordinarily high insurance payments; highly paid workers can be presumed to have more savings to draw on than workers who earn average and below average wages. For example, with a compensation ratio of 50 percent, a worker who previously earned $120,000 but was paid just $60,000 in a new job would be compensated at the ceiling amount of $10,000, since this is lower than the $30,000 that otherwise would be due.

Limits should be placed on benefits for displaced full-time workers who are reemployed in part-time jobs. The purpose of earnings insurance is to compensate trade-displaced workers for part of the wage loss they suffer, not to subsidize a reduction in their weekly hours of employment. One approach is to restrict compensation payments to workers in full-time jobs, that is, in jobs of at least thirty-five regular hours a week. Another approach is to offer sharply lower compensation rates to workers who accept part-time positions.

A crucial element of our plan is that earnings supplements would not be payable until a worker becomes reemployed, and they would cease within a specified period after displacement occurs (say, after two years). Workers who found new jobs early in the two-year period would be eligible for larger total payments than workers who delayed accepting a new job.[17] This provides workers with a strong incentive to search energetically and accept a new job promptly. One of the main reasons that dislocated workers delay serious job search is their failure to accept the fact that the job loss is permanent. By encouraging workers to accept this fact right away, earnings insurance would induce workers to take constructive action to become reemployed as quickly as possible.

State unemployment insurance offices would administer the TAA earnings insurance program, and the federal government would fund benefit payments and administrative costs. Workers would be required to submit pay stubs or other documentary evidence from their current and previous employers to state unemployment offices regularly, in order to obtain timely payments of the employment insurance on a monthly or quarterly basis. The pay stub information would be subject to verification, using the individual earnings records maintained by state unemployment insurance systems.[18]

The advantages of earnings insurance over the current TAA program should be clear. Earnings insurance provides tangible help to a larger percentage of workers suffering trade-induced displacement. It provides compensation for a more important economic loss: the reduction in wages. It offers better incentives. To obtain maximum benefits under the restructured program, workers are encouraged to find new jobs quickly. In contrast, TRA allowances give displaced workers an incentive to delay finding a job.

A critical question is whether to provide earnings insurance to all workers displaced by trade, or only to those displaced by new *trade agreements*. The present TAA program compensates all workers who are displaced by trade. At least initially, we believe that wage insurance should be offered only to workers affected by new trade agreements. Trade is no different than technological change, shifts in consumer

17. Wage insurance would be paid only while an worker remained employed. If a displaced worker obtained a new job but then quit or was laid off, these payments would cease. When the worker became employed once more, the payments would resume but would be limited to the fixed period of eligibility (say, two years) dated from the initial displacement.

18. Earnings of individual workers are reported once every calendar quarter by employers covered by the unemployment insurance system.

tastes, or a variety of other sources of dislocation that cause workers to suffer economic loss. Their losses trigger payments under one or more general purpose safety net programs that have been established to ease the plight of unemployed or poorly paid workers. In contrast, new trade agreements represent specific and identifiable policy actions by the federal government that create well-defined losers and winners. It is both pragmatic and humane for the winners to help to compensate the workers who suffer as a result of a policy change.

We therefore propose that there be a time-limited wage insurance program for each major trade agreement requiring Congressional authorization, that is, for each agreement that requires a change in U.S. law. The resulting legislation would thus include budget authority to provide earnings insurance to workers who will be adversely affected by the new agreement. Congress should scale the amount to the size of dislocation expected from the agreement and the cost of providing the insurance. This cost would be estimated, for budget purposes, by the Congressional Budget Office, taking into account a number of variables: the expected number of displaced workers, the proposed compensation ratio, the length of the compensation period for each insured worker, and the length of time over which adjustment is expected to occur (ordinarily, longer than the period of compensation offered to individual workers).[19]

Consider an example of estimating the cost of earnings insurance. Suppose the administration reached a trade agreement that accelerated the removal of quotas on textile imports. Congressional Budget Office analysts might estimate that one-sixth of the 600,000 American workers currently employed in textiles would be displaced by the agreement, over a four-year period. Displaced workers might be predicted to suffer an average wage loss of 15 percent of their former earnings, or a total of roughly $3,000 per worker per year. (This average reflects the fact that some workers would suffer no wage loss, while others would suffer losses well above $3,000 a year.) Under these assumptions, an earnings insurance program compensating textile workers for

---

19. To minimize the incentive for workers, immediately before a new trade agreement is adopted, to take jobs in industries that potentially will be affected, compensation could be limited to those who had been working in affected industries for some minimum period (say, two years) before the final congressional vote on the new trade agreement.

half of their wage losses over a two-year period following job displacement might cost up to $300 million, with spending spread out over six years (four years of worker displacement from the initiation of the agreement plus an additional two years of insurance eligibility for workers who lose their jobs near the end of this four-year period).

The cost of a wage insurance program that accompanies a sectoral agreement (liberalizing import barriers in only a limited number of industries) is likely to be much easier to estimate than the cost of a program connected with a multilateral agreement (typically affecting many different industrial sectors). For example, the extension of the North American Free Trade Agreement to include all nations in the Western Hemisphere, or a trade agreement between the United States and the Asia Pacific Economic Cooperation nations would affect virtually all industries in which international trade is feasible. Congress could specify in the trade legislation those industries in which displaced workers would be eligible for earnings insurance, thus greatly easing the Congressional Budget Office's burden in deriving cost estimates of the insurance.

The issue of budgeting leads naturally to the question of how wage insurance would be financed and scored for budgetary purposes. While this topic may seem arcane, it is critical for financing federal programs in which year-to-year spending totals are uncertain. Under budget procedures in place since 1990, federal spending is classified as either "mandatory" (for example, social security and medicare) or "discretionary" (for example, grants to build local libraries). Since one goal of wage insurance is to blunt workers' political opposition to liberalized trade, those potentially displaced by a trade agreement must have confidence that any promised assistance will in fact be forthcoming. The only reliable way to accomplish this is to provide the wage insurance payments as an entitlement for all eligible workers and classify the insurance program as mandatory.

Entitlement programs, in turn, must be financed on a "pay-as-you-go" (PAYGO) basis, under current budget rules. If Congress authorizes earnings insurance for a particular class of workers, it must "pay" for the predicted expenditure by either raising taxes or reducing outlays in other entitlement programs. In our experience, in any given year there are numerous potential PAYGO offsets that could finance a wage insurance program of moderate size—including savings in existing entitlement programs, minor tax law changes, and the like. If additional financing is needed, we recommend that it be obtained by slightly increasing a very broad-based tax, such as the personal or corporate income tax. The gains from liberalized trade are widely distributed among U.S. consumers and more narrowly and erratically distributed among U.S. producers. It therefore makes little sense to fund compensation payments by increasing a tax that falls on a narrow class of taxpayers.

Since Congress would specify in advance the industries in which workers could receive earnings insurance compensation, the eligibility determinations would be simpler than under the current TAA program, which requires petitions from workers who believe they have been displaced as a result of trade. Nonetheless, the secretary of labor would still have to determine whether applicants for wage insurance were laid off because of the trade agreement or from some other cause. Although this would not be an easy to determine, it is no more difficult than the determination that must be made under current TAA rules. One way to simplify the task is to make all workers in the designated industries laid off within, say, two years of the enactment of the trade agreement eligible for insurance. Then only after this two-year grace period would the secretary of labor be required to distinguish between trade-related and other causes of displacement. We recognize that this eligibility system might make the program far more costly than a system based on case-by-case determinations. But by assuring potentially displaced workers in advance that they will be eligible for earnings insurance, it can lessen workers' political opposition to trade liberalization.

In comparison with the present TAA program, earnings insurance provides much more valuable compensation to workers who lose out as a result of freer trade, and it offers this compensation in a way that greatly improves the incentives for speedy adjustment. To be sure, this kind of insurance offers far more valuable protection to middle-class workers than it does to the poorly paid. Most middle-class workers earn decent wages in their current jobs, so their wages have a long way to fall when they are displaced as a result of trade. A worker earning the minimum wage cannot suffer a loss in hourly pay as a result of displacement; that worker's next job will pay no less than the minimum wage. Earnings insurance thus has no value to the minimum-wage worker.

In our view, however, this is not a deficiency of the proposal. Unemployment insurance payments are also pegged to a worker's previous salary, and higher wage workers receive more generous weekly benefits. The purpose of both types of insurance is to replace part of the earnings lost as a result of the event that is insured against. Unemployment insurance replaces part of the earnings lost as a result of unemployment; earnings insurance replaces part of earnings lost as a result of a worker's acceptance of a lower wage job. If a displaced worker earning $7.50 an hour quickly finds another job that pays $7.50 an hour, the worker has suffered little loss from displacement. If a worker earning $10.00 an hour must accept a job that pays $7.50 an hour, that worker has lost $2.50 an hour—25 percent of the previous wage. Complaining that the second worker receives more favorable treatment than the first is a little like criticizing automobile insurance because larger settlements are paid when a car is totaled than when it is dented.

Some will question the fairness of restricting earnings insurance to workers injured as a result of new trade agreements. Workers who suffer job loss as a result of other kinds of structural change surely believe their situation justifies compensation, too. Coal miners would think they deserved recompense if tougher environmental regulations dried up the market for American coal. Bank tellers might want compensation if their jobs were eliminated by automatic teller machines. It is not easy to know where to draw the line. Because this book is devoted to global economic integration, we naturally emphasize compensating workers who are adversely affected when the nation adopts new trading or investment rules that lead to freer world markets. But we are sympathetic with the claims of other classes of workers who are hurt by the process of change. If earnings insurance turns out to be workable, and is effective in helping displaced workers adjust to trade-related change, there is a sound case for expanding this insurance to cover a broader group of displaced workers.[20]

---

20. In that event, it may be justifiable to finance the program by adding to the unemployment insurance tax, since, theoretically, many workers could be in a position to collect the insurance at some point in their careers. This is not the case with a narrowly crafted wage insurance program targeted only at the small class of workers potentially displaced by new trade agreements.

Conclusion

The United States' postwar policy of openness has brought enormous benefits to the nation and to others around the world. Those benefits are threatened, however, by a rising chorus of complaints about the impact of globalization and the policies that have helped to make world economic integration possible. While most of these complaints lack hard empirical support, they resonate with many Americans because of widespread concern about slow income growth, widening inequality, and worker dislocation. In addition, a few of the complaints do have basis in fact. Global integration has contributed to a small degree to the increase in wage disparities. Liberalized trade rules generate losses for some companies and workers and, in the short run, can contribute to greater joblessness.

Those of us who wish to maintain or expand open trade and investment have an obligation to address the legitimate concerns of workers and companies who can be hurt by freer trade. The combination of proposals described in this chapter offers a modest, practical, and humane course of action.

REFERENCES

Ackerman, Bruce, and Anne Alstot. 1998. *The Stakeholder Society.* Yale University Press. Forthcoming.

APEC. 1994. "Economic Leaders' Declaration of Common Resolve." Bongor, Indonesia. November 15.

Baily, Martin N. 1993. "Manufacturing Productivity." Washington, D.C.: McKinsey Global Institute.

Baily, Martin Neil, Gary Burtless, and Robert E. Litan. 1993. *Growth with Equity.* Brookings.

Bayard, Thomas O., and Kimberly Ann Elliot. 1994. *Reciprocity and Retaliation in U.S. Trade Policy.* Washington D.C.: Institute for International Economics.

Bennefield, Robert L. 1997. "Health Insurance Coverage: 1996." Current Population Reports, Census Bureau. September. Series P60-199.

Bhagwati, Jagdish. 1997. "Fast Track to Nowhere." The *Economist* (October 18): 21–23.

Bhagwati, Jagdish, and Robert E. Hudec, eds. 1996. *Fair Trade and Harmonization: Prerequisites for Free Trade?* MIT Press.

Bhagwati, Jagdish, and T. N. Srinivasan. 1996. "Trade and the Environment: Does Environmental Diversity Detract from the Case for Free Trade?" In *Fair Trade and Harmonization: Prerequisities for Free Trade?* edited by Jagdish Bhagwati and Robert E. Hudec, 159–224. MIT Press.

Borjas, George J., Richard B. Freeman, and Lawrence F. Katz. 1997. "How Much Do Immigration and Trade Affect Labor Market Outcomes?" *Brookings Papers on Economic Activity, 1997:1*: 1–67.

Brainard, S. Lael, and David A. Riker. 1997. "Are U.S. Multinationals Exporting U.S. Jobs?" Working Paper 5958. Cambridge, Mass.: National Bureau of Economic Research.

Council of Economic Advisers. Various years. *Economic Report of the President.*

Dam, Kenneth W. 1970. *The GATT; Law and International Economic Organization.* University of Chicago Press.

Decker, Paul T., and Walter Corson. 1995. "International Trade and Worker Displacement: Evaluation of the Trade Adjustment Assistance Program." *Industrial and Labor Relations Review*: 48 (July): 758–74.

Elliot, Hugh S.R., ed. 1910. *The Letters of John Stuart Mill.* 2 vols. London: Longmans, Green.

Faiola, Anthony. 1997. "Chile Takes Its Trade Elsewhere: Delay of U.S. 'Fast Track' Legislation Makes Canadian and Mexican Products More Attractive." *Washington Post,* December 25, A29.

Federal Reserve Bank at Washington. 1997. *Federal Reserve Bulletin* (May).

Frankel, Jeffrey A., with Ernesto Stein and Shang-Jin Wei. 1997. *Regional Trading Blocs in the World Economic System.* Washington, D.C.: Institute for International Economics.

Freeman, Richard B. 1997. *When Earnings Diverge: Causes, Consequences, and Cures for the New Inequality in the U.S.* Washington, D.C.: National Planning Association.

General Agreement on Tariffs and Trade. 1952. *Basic Instruments and Selected Documents. Volume 1: Text of the Agreement and Other Instruments and Procedures.* Geneva.

_____. 1984/85, 1995. *International Trade.* Geneva.

Goldstein, Morris. 1997. *The Case for an International Banking Standard.* Washington, D.C.: Institute for International Economics.

Golub, Stephen S. 1997. "International Labor Standards and International Trade." IMF Working Paper 97/37.

Greenberger, Robert S., Laura Johannes, and Ross Kerber. 1997. "WTO's Kodak Ruling Heightens Trade Tensions." *Wall Street Journal,* December 8, p. A3.

Greider, William. 1997. *One World, Ready or Not: The Manic Logic of Global Capitalism.* Simon & Schuster.

International Monetary Fund. Various years. *Direction of Trade Statistics Yearbook.*

Jacobson, Louis S., Robert J. LaLonde, and Daniel G. Sullivan. 1992. "Earnings Losses of Displaced Workers." *American Economic Review* 83 (September) 685–709.

_____. 1993. *The Costs of Worker Dislocation.* Kalamazoo, Mich.: W. E. Upjohn Institute of Employment Research, 1993).

Jaffe, Adam B., and others. 1995. "Environmental Regulation and the Competitiveness of U.S. Manufacturing." *Journal of Economic Literature* (March): 132–63.

Koretz, Gene. 1997. "The Unhealthy U.S. Income Gap." *Business Week* (November 10): 22.

Krugman, Paul. 1997a. "A Raspberry for Free Trade: Protectionists Serve up Tainted Fruit and Red Herrings." *Slate* (November 20).

———. 1997b. "What Should Trade Negotiators Negotiate About?" *Journal of Economic Literature* 35 (March): 113–20.

Lawrence, Robert Z. 1996. *Single World, Divided Nations? International Trade and the OECD Labor Markets.* Brookings/OECD.

Lawrence, Robert Z., Albert Bressand, and Takatoshi Ito. 1996. *A Vision for the World Economy: Openness, Diversity, and Cohesion.* Brookings.

Lawrence, Robert Z., and Robert E. Litan. 1986. *Saving Free Trade: A Pragmatic Approach.* Brookings.

Lawrence, Robert Z., and Matthew J. Slaughter. 1993. "International Trade and American Wages in the 1980s: Giant Sucking Sound or Small Hiccup?" *Brookings Papers on Economic Activity: Microeconomics 1993:* 2: 161–210.

Leamer, Edward E. 1996. "In Search of Stolper-Samuelson Effects on U.S. Wages." Working Paper 5427. Cambridge, Mass.: National Bureau of Economic Research.

Leigh, Duane E. 1989. *Assisting Displaced Workers: Do the States Have a Better Idea?* Kalamazoo, Mich.: W. E. Upjohn Institute for Employment Research.

———. 1991. "Public Policy to Retrain Displaced Workers: What Does the Record Show?" In *Job Displacement: Consequences and Implications for Policy,* edited by John T. Addison, 244–78. Wayne State University Press.

Levy, Frank, and Richard J. Murnane. 1992. "U.S. Earnings Levels and Earnings Inequality: A Review of Recent Trends and Proposed Explanations." *Journal of Economic Literature* 30 (September): 1333–81.

Litan, Robert E., and William Niskanen. 1998. *Going Digital!* Brookings and Cato.

Mankiw, N. Gregory. 1997. *Principles of Economics.* Fort Worth: Dryden, Harcourt Brace.

Mill, John Stuart. 1909. *Principles of Political Economy,* edited with an introduction by William James Ashley. London: Longmans, Green.

Nader, Ralph, and Lori Wallach. 1996. "GATT, NAFTA, and the Subversion of the Democratic Process." In *The Case against the Global Economy: And for a Turn toward the Local,* edited by Jerry Mander and Edward Goldsmith. San Francisco: Sierra Club Books.

Phelps, Edmund S. 1997. *Rewarding Work: How to Restore Participation and Self-Support to Free Enterprise.* Harvard University Press.

Quinlan, Joseph P. 1997a. "Global Engagement: Understanding How U.S. Companies Compete in the World Economy." *U.S. and the Americas Investment Research.* December 24. Morgan Stanley Dean Witter.

_____. 1997b. "The 'Sucking Sound' Revisited—Assessing the Import Demand of Developing Nations." Morgan Stanley Dean Witter, International Investment Research, September 24.

Richardson, David J., and Karin Rindal. 1996. *Why Exports Matter: More!* Washington, D.C.: Institute for International Economics and the Manufacturing Institute.

Riker, David A., and S. Lael Brainard. 1997. "U.S. Multinationals and Competition from Low Wage Countries." Working Paper 5959. Cambridge, Mass.: National Bureau of Economic Research.

Rodrik, Dani. 1997. "Sense and Nonsense in the Globalization Debate." *Foreign Policy* 107 (Summer): 19–36.

Sachs, Jeffrey D., and Howard J. Shatz. 1994. "Trade and Jobs in U.S. Manufacturing." *Brookings Papers on Economic Activity:1*: 1–69.

Samuelson, Paul A. 1948. *Economics, An Introductory Analysis*. McGraw-Hill.

Schott, Jeffrey J., ed. 1996. *The World Trading System: Challenges Ahead*. Washington, D.C.: Institute for International Economics.

Slaughter, Matthew J., and Phillip Swagel. 1997. "The Effect of Globalization on Wages in the Advanced Economies." IMF Working Paper WP/97/43.

Smith, James P., and Barry Edmonston, eds. 1997. *The New Americans: Economic, Demographic, and Fiscal Effects of Immigration*. National Academy of Sciences.

Stolper, Wolfgang, and Paul A. Samuelson. 1941. "Protection and Real Ages." *Review of Economic Studies* (November): 58–73.

Sykes, Alan O. 1995. *Product Standards for Internationally Integrated Goods Markets*. Brookings.

Thurow, Lester C. 1992. *Head to Head: The Coming Economic Battle among Japan, Europe, and America*. New York: Morrow.

U.S. Department of Commerce, Bureau of Economic Analysis. 1997. *Survey of Current Business* 77 (October).

U.S. Department of Labor, Bureau of Labor Statistics. 1997. "Productivity and Costs, Second Quarter 1997." News Release 97-272.

U.S. Department of the Treasury. 1892. *Alexander Hamilton's Famous Report on Manufacturers: Made to Congress December 5, 1791, in His Capacity as Secretary of the Treasury*. Boston: Potter.

_____. 1984, 1988, 1997. *Statistical Abstract of the United States*.

USTR (United States Special Trade Representative). 1996. *The President's 1996 Annual Report on the Trade Agreements Program*.

Werner, Ingrid M., and Linda L. Tesar. 1998. "The Internationalization of Securities Markets since the 1987 Crash." *Brookings-Wharton Papers on Financial Services 1998*. Brookings. (forthcoming).

Wilson, John Douglas. 1996. "Capital Mobility and Environmental Standards: Is There a Theoretical Basis for a Race to the Bottom?" In *Fair Trade and*

Harmonization: Prerequisites for Free Trade? edited by Jagdish Bhagwati and Robert E. Hudec, 393–428. MIT Press.

Woodward, Bob. 1994. *The Agenda: Inside the Clinton White House.* Simon & Schuster.

World Bank. 1995. *Workers in an Integrating World*, World Development Report 1995.

World Trade Organization. Various years. *Annual Report.*

INDEX

Ackerman, Bruce, 131
Adams, John, 42
Advanced Technology Program (ATP), 99*n*6
Africa (South), 112
Alstot, Anne, 131
Antidumping. *See* Dumping
Antitrust issues, 23, 140
APEC. *See* Asia Pacific Economic Cooperation forum
Articles *19* and *20*. *See* General Agreement on Tariffs and Trade
Asian currency crisis of *1997*: causes, 36, 112; effects, 21–22, 47, 75; trade issues, 103, 107
Asia Pacific Economic Cooperation forum (APEC), 31–32
ATP. *See* Advanced Technology Program

Bastiat, Frederic, 27
Benefits, employment. *See* Economic issues
Boskin Report on the Bureau of Labor Statistics' Consumer Price Index, 64
Buchanan, Patrick, 6

Canada: exports to the United States, 16; investment in the United States, 35–36; free trade agreements, 31, 32, 56; United States investment in, 85.

See also North American Free Trade Agreement
Carville, James, 110
Chile, 32
China, 100
Clay, Henry, 24–25
Clinton (Bill) administration, 31–32, 99*n*6, 120–21, 136
Coal mining, 124
Cold war, 11, 24, 72
Committee on Trade Agreements, 28*n*5
Communications. *See* Technology
Comparative advantage, 19–20, 47, 96
Compensation. *See* Wages and compensation
Competition: effects of protectionism, 26; effects of trade, 21, 23; effects on wages, 65, 71; pricing, 102; unfairness in, 90
Concorde, 26
Congressional Budget Office, 146
Constitution, U.S., 13–14, 119, 138
Consumer Price Index (CPI), 64, 77
Consumers: benefits from trade, 20–21, 22, 30; consumption of manufactured goods, 52, 72; effects of Asian crisis, 107; trade sanctions, 125
Corson, Walter, 143
CPI. *See* Consumer Price Index
Cuba, 112

Globalization: of capital flows, 35–36, 62, 110–11; cultural, 117; economic performance and, 4; effects of, 89, 112–17, 150; "global glut," 71–72, 73, 75; measures of, 5; national sovereignty and, 112–20; productivity and, 63, 64; regulations and standards, 115–16; wages and, 65. *See also* Trade agreements; United States
Globalization, criticism: business relocations, 110–11; effects on trade, 21, 71–72; effects on the United States, 42–43, 59, 127; general arguments, 11; public opposition, 6
Great Britain. *See* England
Great Depression, 49, 132
Greenspan, Alan, 1
Greider, William, 71–72

Hamilton, Alexander, 24–25, 42, 98
Hawley-Smoot Tariff Act of 1930, 28, 49
Health care issues, 112–14, 115*n*3, 135–37
Hecksher, Eli, 61–62, 84
Hong Kong, 28
Human rights, 112

ILO. *See* International Labor Organization
IMF. *See* International Monetary Fund
Immigration: effects of, 4, 41–42, 71, 87; labor standards, 121*n*12; skill and education of immigrants, 86–87
Imports. *See* Exports and imports
Income. *See* Economic issues; Wages and compensation
Indonesia, 99
Inflation. *See* Economic issues
Innovation, 23–24
Insurance. *See* Employment; Health care issues
Intellectual property, 101, 122
Interest rates. *See* Economic issues
International Labor Organization (ILO), 121, 125
International Monetary Fund (IMF), 37, 99, 129
International Trade Commission (ITC), 138
Internet. *See* Technology

Investment, domestic, 85, 105–07
Investment, foreign: effects of, 4, 7, 35, 84–85, 88; foreign trade and, 33–38; free trade and, 96, 115; multinational companies, 39–40, 45; portfolio and direct, 34–35, 38, 116; regulations and, 115. *See also* United States
Israel, 31
Italy, 19. *See also* Europe (Western)
ITC. *See* International Trade Commission

Japan: automobile industry, 14–15; current account surplus, 105; exports to the United States, 15–16, 108–09; imports from the United States, 108–09; investment in the United States, 35; tariffs, 32, 108–09; television industry, 26; trade surplus, 103–04; trading practices, 90, 99, 101; United States investment in, 85; wages, 124–25
Jordan, Michael, 20

Kennedy, John F., 27
Kodak, 101
Korea (South), 99, 125
Krugman, Paul, 124–25
Kyoto agreement, 95

Labor issues, 120–22, 124–25
Latin America, 16, 27–28
Lincoln, Abraham, 24–25
List, Friedrich, 25

Management, 35
Mankiw, Gregory, 20
Manufacturing. *See* Employment
Mercosur trade arrangement, 31, 32
Mexico: currency crisis, 36, 57, 103, 129; exports to the United States, 15–16; free trade agreements, 31, 32, 56; tariffs, 56; United States investment in, 85. *See also* North American Free Trade Agreement
MFN issues (Most favored nation issues). *See* Trade agreements and free trade
Mill, John Stuart, 25
Mondale, Walter, 62
Monopoly power, 96
Morgan Stanley Dean Witter, 72–73